NOTES ON THIS SERIES OF SIGNALLING DIAGRAMS

GENERAL

This volume is one of a series that will eventually cover much of the west country and Southern England, and will make public the author's vast collection of data.

The published information represents many years of research, but even so, some signal boxes - notably those closed in the 1930's, seem to have vanished without leaving any official records.

The collection cannot therefore claim to be complete, although in some areas total coverage has been possible.

The amount of information also varies widely from place to place, and the listed alterations do not represent a full history of the signal boxes in most cases.

For small layouts where the alterations have been few, one diagram with suitable notes is usually sufficient, but at locations that have undergone considerable remodelling several drawings are necessary.

The diagrams are arranged in line order, starting from the furthest point from London for all main lines. For branches the sequence is the same if the line has a junction with the main line that allows through running from London, but if the junction faces the other direction the drawings are arranged from the main line to the terminus.

The quoted opening and closing dates of signal boxes call for some explanation, as it must not be thought that they were necessarily manned continuously over that period. Those boxes fitted with a closing switch were often closed regularly at night or on Sundays, and some were in fact switched out permanently for long periods before their final abolition.

The "opening" date is therefore that on which the equipment was officially brought into use, and the "closing" date indicates when the signals, instruments etc. were removed or made inoperative by the Signal Engineer.

SIGNALS

These are drawn parallel to the track, facing the direction to which they apply. Although the configuration is represented as accurately as possible, no attempt is made to differentiate between tall and short signal posts except in a few cases where these dimensions are extreme.

Signal arms and discs are depicted in the "normal" position - usually at Danger/Caution. Whenever possible, the distance of each running signal from the centre of the controlling signal box is given in yards. Some former SR box diagrams give full distance tables for points and signals.

POINTS

Points controlled from a lever frame or panel are drawn to the split-line format, the position in which they lie when the lever is normal in the frame being shown by the continuous line. Points which do not connect with a running line are often worked by individual hand levers and have no recognised "normal" and "reverse", and are therefore shown differently (see symbols page).

TRACK CIRCUITS & TREADLES

These are either numbered according to function (2AT - signal 2 Approach Track) lettered singly on small layouts (A,B,C, etc.) or lettered in a progressive sequence (AA, AB, AC, BB, BC, etc.).

Where both track circuits and treadles are present, the treadle letters are shown plain and those applying to track circuits enclosed in a circle. In coloured light areas the overlap of each track circuit beyond the signals is given thus: "OL 440".

GROUND FRAMES

Ground Frames are provided to work points or level crossings too far from the signal box for direct observation by the signalman or beyond the distance limit for mechanical operation. Their functions are always released from the controlling signal box, and several methods of doing this are to be found. The most common are the S.R. standard electrical release lever (ELEC REL) and the mechanical release (MECH REL), but Annett's keys were much favoured by the G.W.R.

The lever numbers of ground frames (where known) are written within a distinctive shape - a circle, square, triangle etc. - to avoid confusion with numbers in the main signal box lever frame.

ACKNOWLEDGMENTS

The assistance of various members of the Signalling Record Society, particularly D. Collins and C. Osment is gratefully acknowledged in the preparation of this series.

INDEX TO LOCATIONS IN VOLUME 3

ASHCOTT	48	LAMYATT CROSSING	19
BASON BRIDGE	45	MASBURY	12
BAILEY GATE	34/35	MIDFORD	3
BAILEY GATE CROSSING	36	MIDSOMER NORTON (SOUTH)	8
BATH STATION	1	MOOREWOOD	10
BATH JUNCTION	2	POLSHAM	56
BINEGAR	11	PYLLE	51
BLANDFORD	30/31/32	RADSTOCK EAST	6
BRIDGWATER NORTH	53	RADSTOCK WEST	7
BRUTON ROAD CROSSING	19	SHAPWICK	47
BURNHAM-ON-SEA	39	SHEPTON MALLET	14
CHILCOMPTON	9	SHILLINGSTONE	28
COLE	20	SPETISBURY	33
COSSINGTON	54	STALBRIDGE	26
CORFE MULLEN JCN	37	STOURPAINE	29
EDINGTON JCN	46	STURMINSTER NEWTON	27
EVERCREECH JCN NORTH	16/17	TEMPLECOMBE 'B'	24
EVERCREECH JCN SOUTH	18	TEMPLECOMBE - No. 3 JCN	22
EVERCREECH NEW	15	TEMPLECOMBE JCN	23
GLASTONBURY & STREET	49	WELLOW	4
HENSTRIDGE	25	WELLS 'A'	57/58/59
HIGHBRIDGE 'A'	42	WEST PENNARD	50
HIGHBRIDGE 'B'	41	WINCANTON	21
HIGHBRIDGE 'C' ('A' from 1936)	40	WINSOR HILL	13
HIGHBRIDGE - LOCO ('A' from 1936) (EAST 'C' from c1949)	43/44	WRITHINGTON	5

The remainder of the route covered by S&D trains is dealt with in volume 2 "The SR in East Dorset".

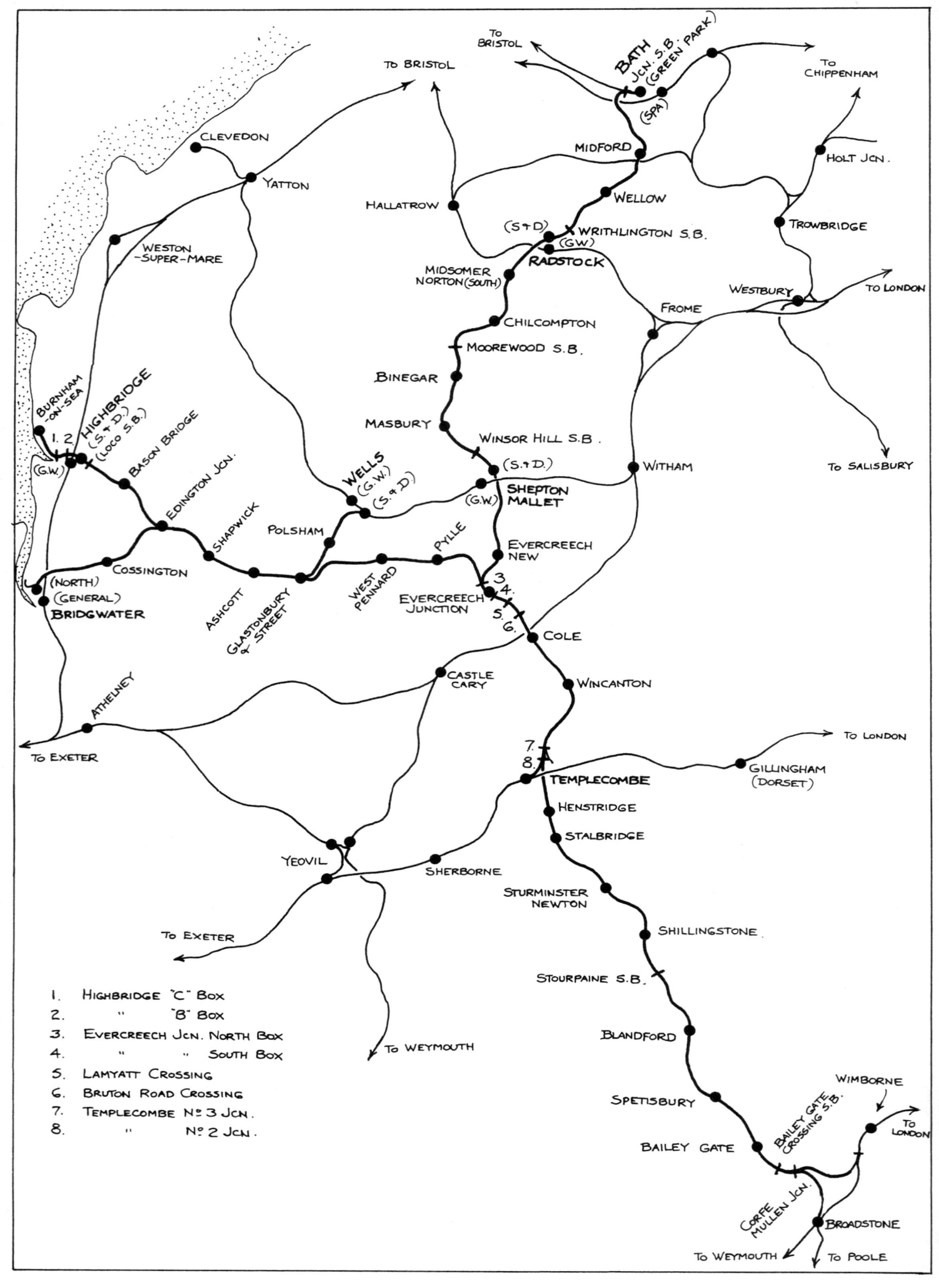

SECTION ONE

BATH (GREEN PARK) TO BROADSTONE

NOTE: FROM 1874 THIS ROUTE FORMED THE "MAIN LINE" OF THE SOMERSET & DORSET, THE ORIGINAL SECTION OF LINE BETWEEN HIGHBRIDGE AND EVERCREECH JCN. BEING RELEGATED TO BRANCH LINE STATUS.

LINE OPENED AS FOLLOWS:

WIMBORNE TO BLANDFORD 01-11-1860
EVERCREECH TO TEMPLECOMBE 03-02-1862
(As part of line from Glastonbury)
TEMPLECOMBE TO BLANDFORD 31-07-1863
BATH TO EVERCREECH JCN. 20-07-1874
CORFE MULLEN TO BROADSTONE 14-12-1885*

*The physical junction was at Bailey Gate until 1905.

LINE CLOSED AS FOLLOWS:

CORFE MULLEN TO WIMBORNE 11-07-1920 (Pass.) & 17-06-1933 (Goods). TO PASSENGERS THROUGHOUT ON 07-03-1966 (Last train previous day) AND TO ALL TRAFFIC BETWEEN BATH AND WRITHLINGTON AND RADSTOCK AND BLANDFORD FORUM. NEW CHORD OPENED AT RADSTOCK BETWEEN FORMER GWR LINE AND S & D TO PROVIDE ACCESS TO WRITHLINGTON COLLIERY. BROADSTONE TO BLANDFORD FORUM CLOSED COMPLETELY 06-03-1966. RADSTOCK TO WRITHLINGTON COLLIERY CLOSED 19-11-1973.

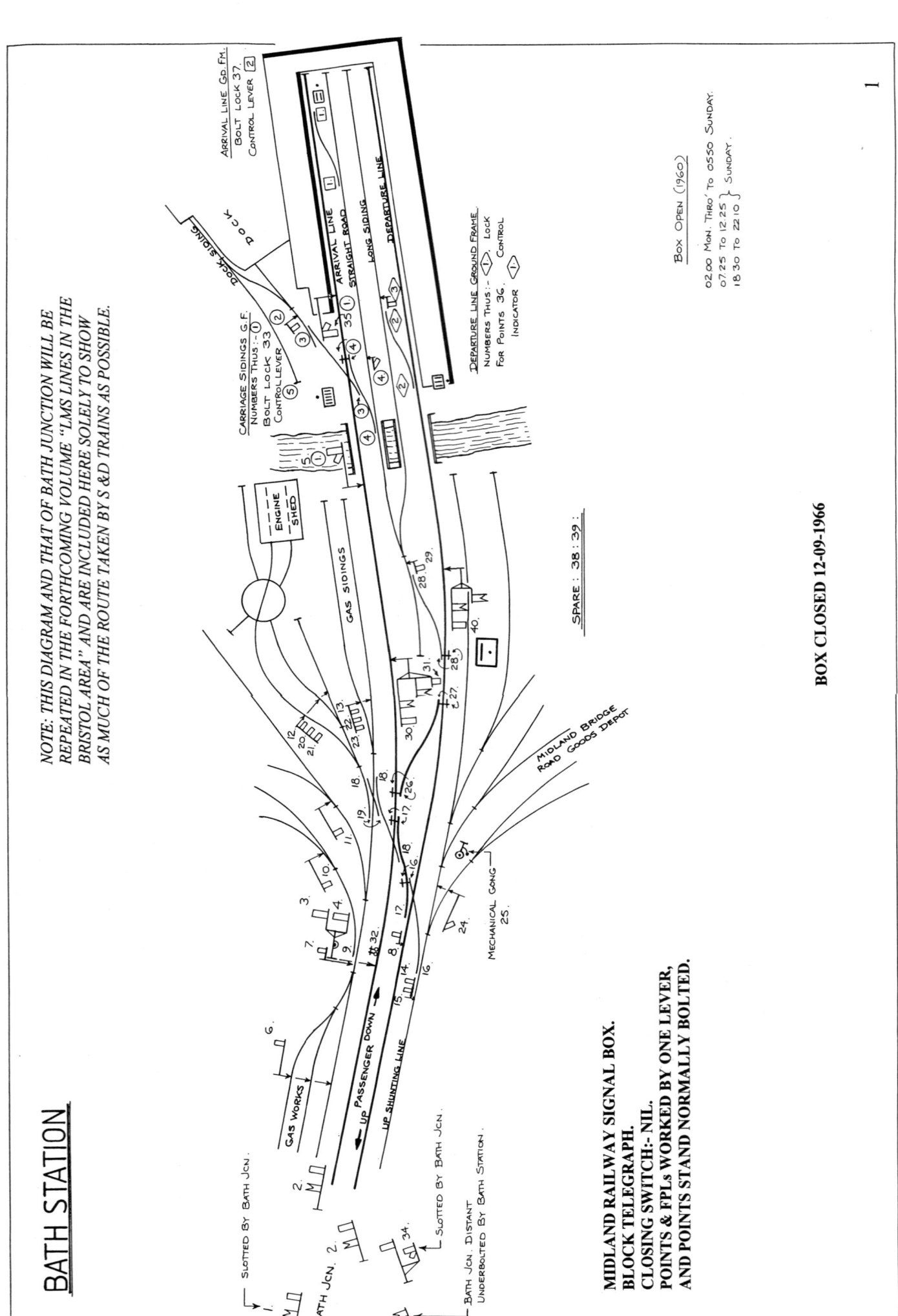

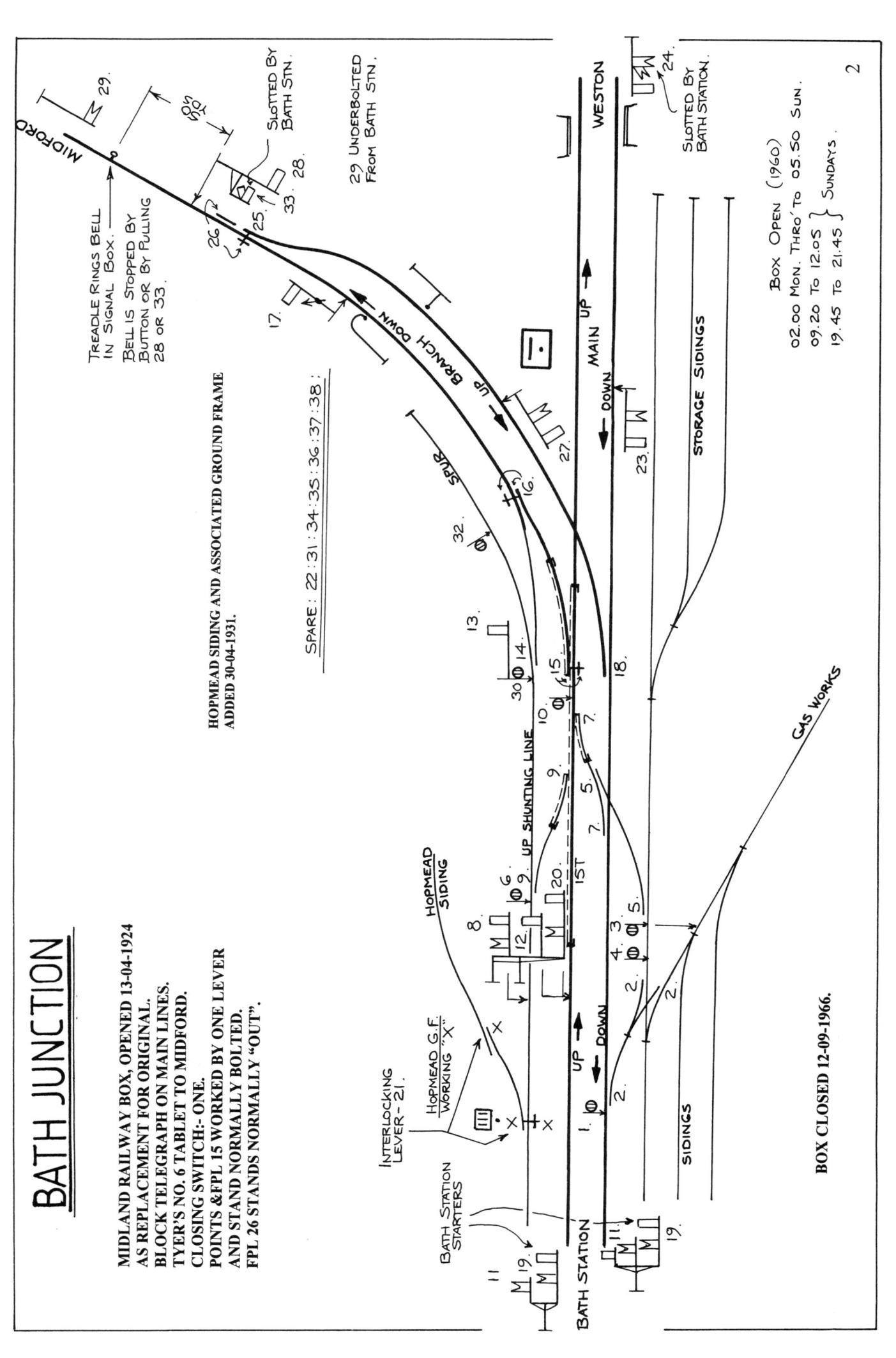

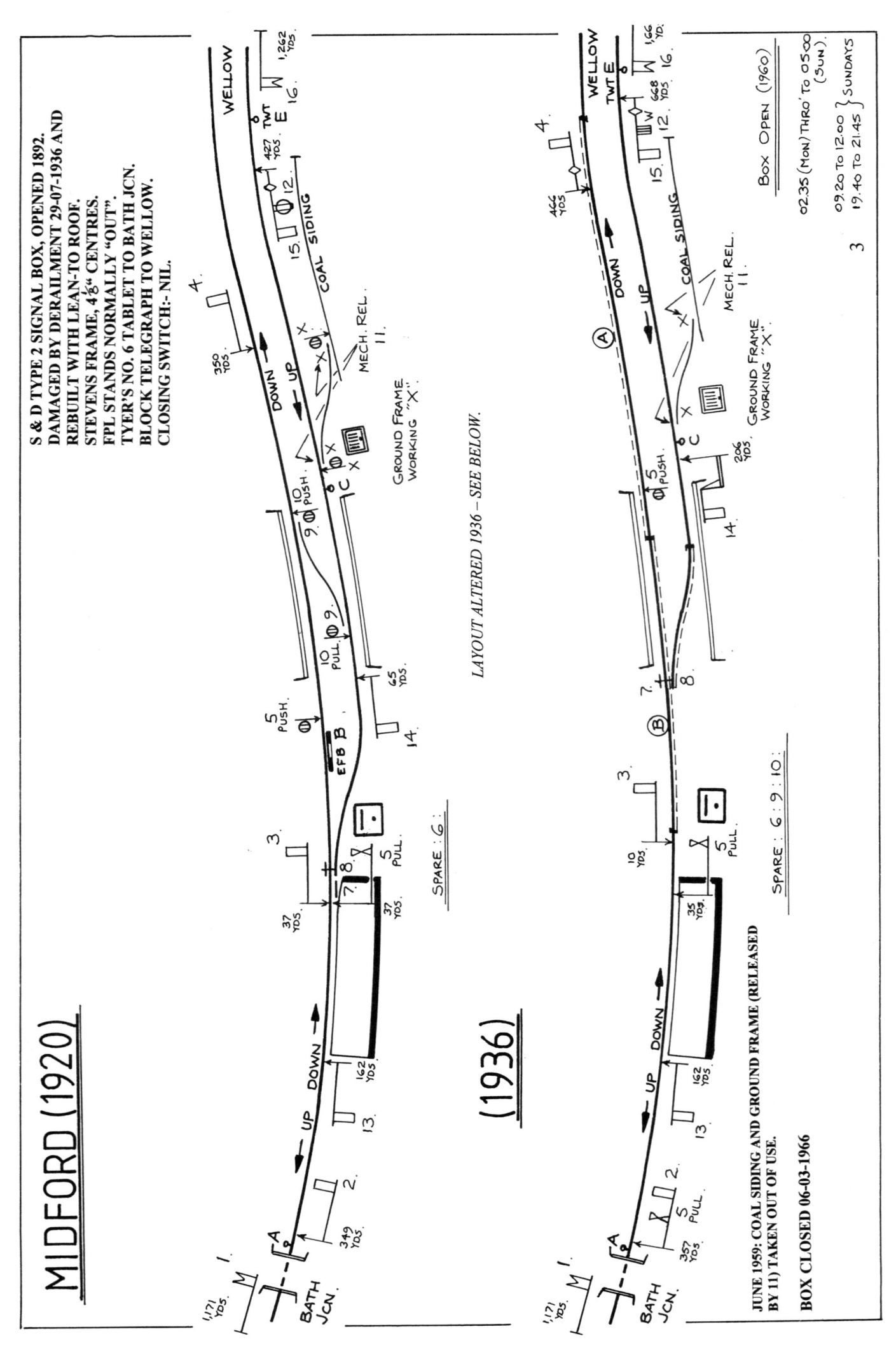

WELLOW

**S & D TYPE 2 SIGNAL BOX, OPENED 1894.
STEVENS FRAME, 4⅛" CENTRES.
BLOCK TELEGRAPH.
CLOSING SWITCH:- ONE.**

SPARE: 8 : 9 : 12.

Gate Lock - 1.
Wickets - 2.

Ground Frame Numbers Thus:- ①

30-06-1964: GROUND FRAME AND ASSOCIATED CONNECTIONS ABOLISHED. LEVERS 14 AND 14 MADE SPARE.

BOX CLOSED 06-03-1966

Box Open (1960)
06.10 to 20.40 (Mon. to Sat.)
Closed Sundays.

WRITHLINGTON

S & D TYPE 2 SIGNAL BOX, OPENED 01-07-1894
TO REPLACE BRAYSDOWN COLLIERY BOX.
STEVENS FRAME, 4⅛" CENTRES.

BLOCK TELEGRAPH.
CLOSING SWITCH:- ONE.

13-04-1962: POINTS 5 AND DISCS 4 PULL & 4 PUSH
TAKEN OUT OF USE.

SPARE : 10 : 11 : 12 : 13 : 16 :

BOX CLOSED 06-03-1966 AND REMAINING CONNECTIONS
CONVERTED TO HAND OPERATION. LINE WORKED AS
SIDING FROM RADSTOCK.

Box Open (1960)
08.00 to 15.10 Mondays
06.30 to 13.40 Tues - Sats.
Closed Sundays.

RADSTOCK EAST

RENAMED "RADSTOCK NORTH 'A'" 1951.

S & D TYPE 2 SIGNAL BOX, OPENED 1894.
STEVENS FRAME, 4⅛" CENTRES.
BLOCK TELEGRAPH.
CLOSING SWITCH: ONE.

12-02-1961: POINTS 11 AND DISCS 8 PULL & 8 PUSH TAKEN OUT OF USE.

SPARE : 4 : 5 : 13 : 14 :

Box Open (1960)
06.40 to 21.10 Mon. to Sat.
Closed Sunday.

BOX CLOSED 14-08-1964.

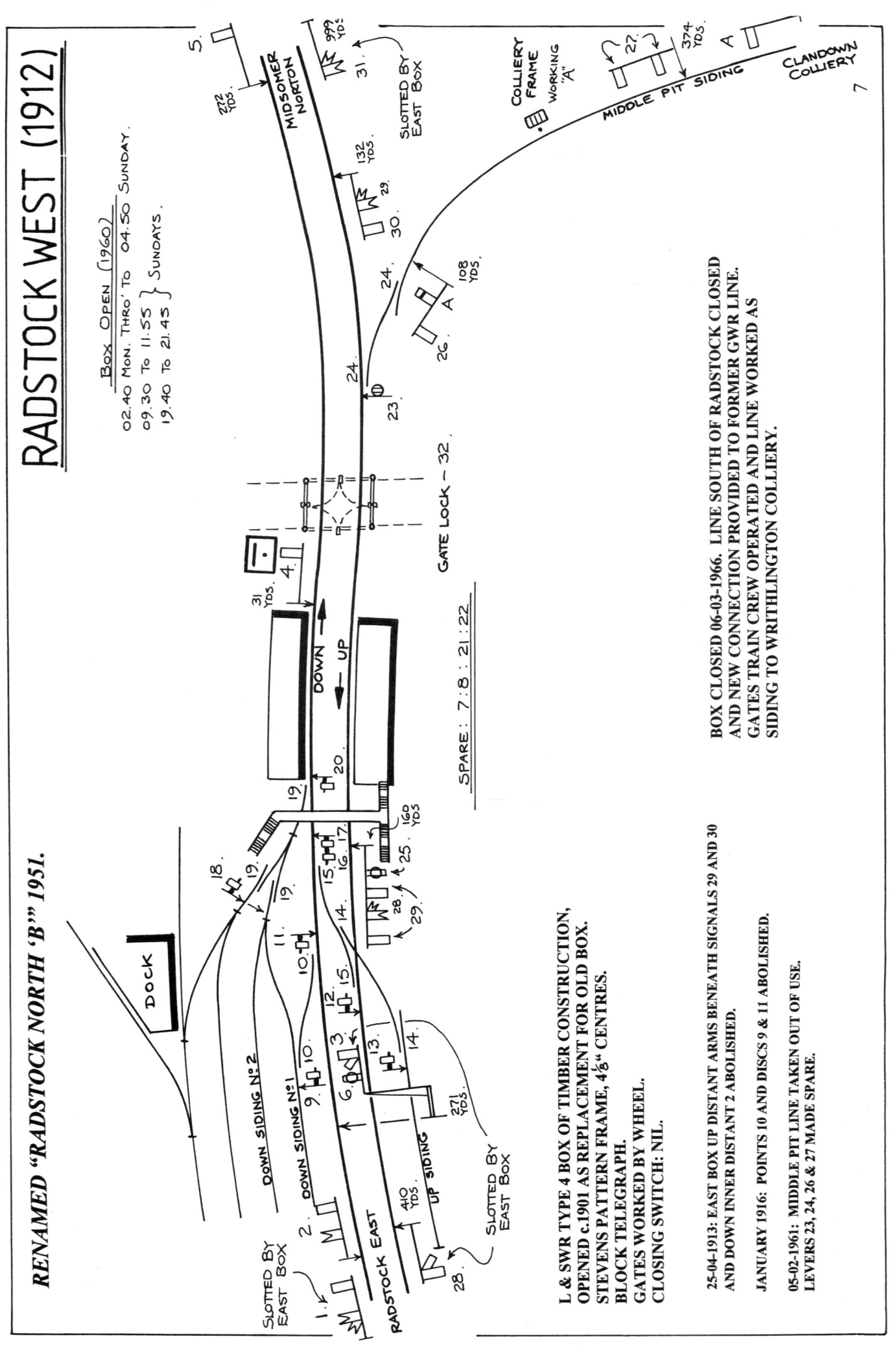

MIDSOMER NORTON

"MIDSOMER NORTON SOUTH" FROM 1949.

S & D TYPE 2 SIGNAL BOX, OPENED c.1890.
STEVENS FRAME, 4⅛" CENTRES.
BLOCK TELEGRAPH.
CLOSING SWITCH: ONE.

SOUTH GROUND FRAME AND TRAP POINTS BROUGHT
INTO USE 21-03-1907.

BOX CLOSED 06-03-1966. LINE CLOSED.

SPARE : 9.

Box Open (1960)
06.40 to 21.10 (Mon. to Sat.)
Closed Sundays.

8

CHILCOMPTON

S & D TYPE 2 SIGNAL BOX, OPENED c. 1890.
STEVENS PATTERN FRAME, 4⅛" CENTRES.
BLOCK TELEGRAPH.
CLOSING SWITCH:- ONE.

BOX CLOSED 11-04-1965

Box Open (1960)

06.40 to 21.10 (Mon. to Sat.)
Closed Sunday.

MOOREWOOD

L & SWR TYPE 4 – STYLE BOX, OPENED 1914.
STEVENS PATTERN FRAME, 4⅛" CENTRES.
BLOCK TELEGRAPH.
CLOSING SWITCH:- ONE.

09-12-1964: DOWN SIDINGS TAKEN OUT OF USE.
LEVERS 11, 12, & 13 MADE SPARE.

BOX CLOSED 05-07-1965.

Runaway Spring Points 983 yards

Box Open (1960)
07.20 to 13.15 Mon. to Sat.
Closed Sunday.

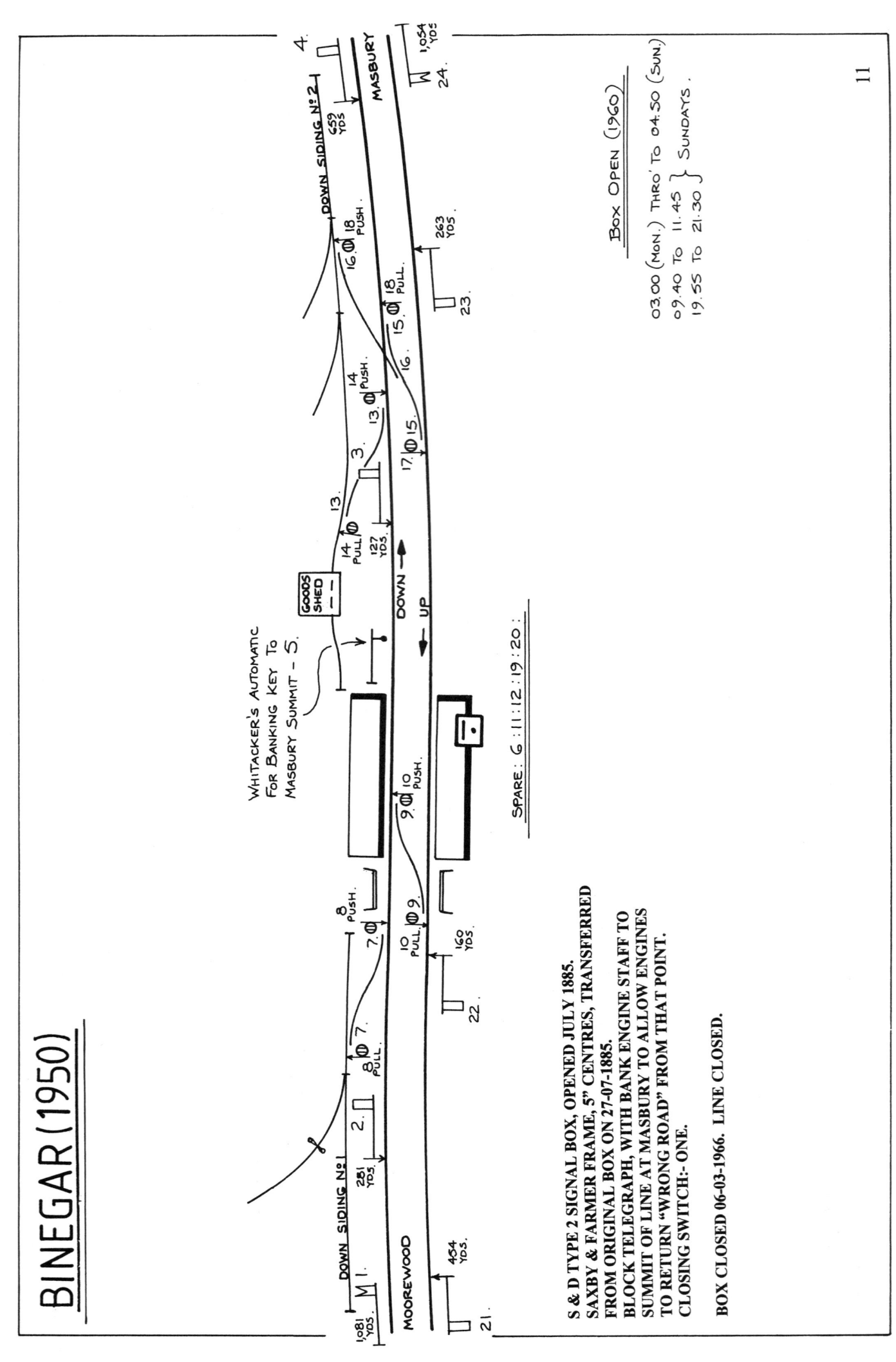

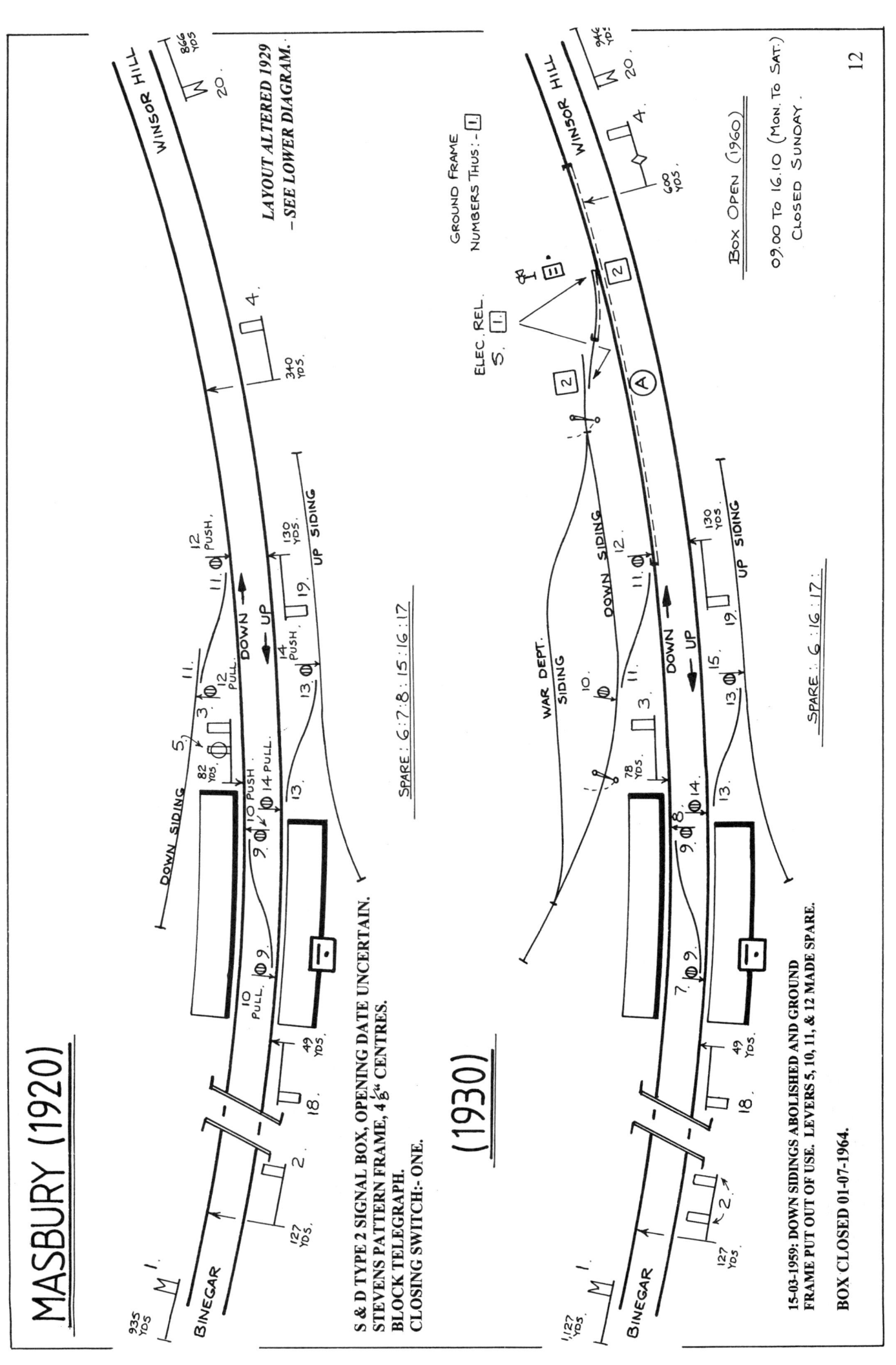

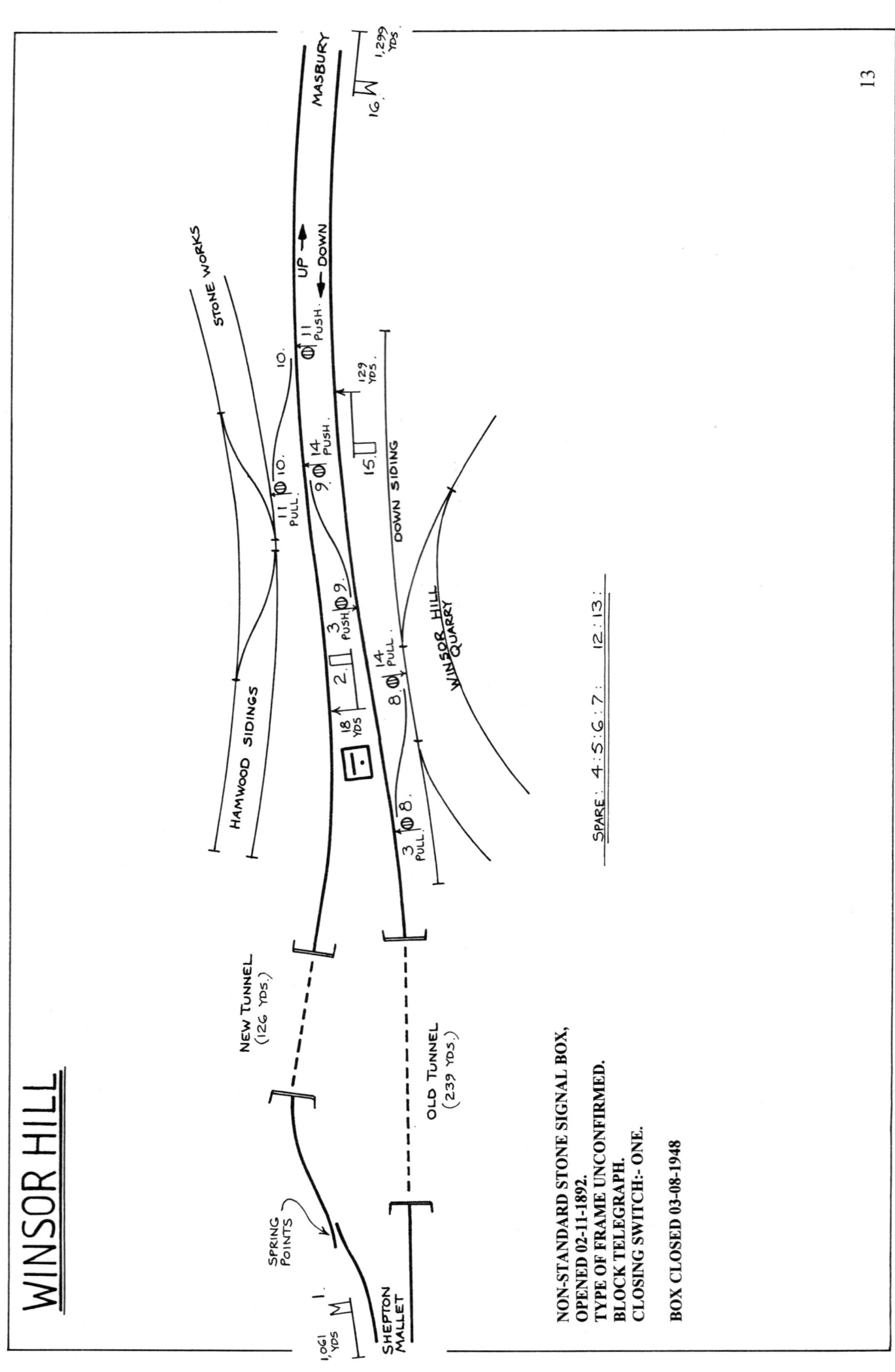

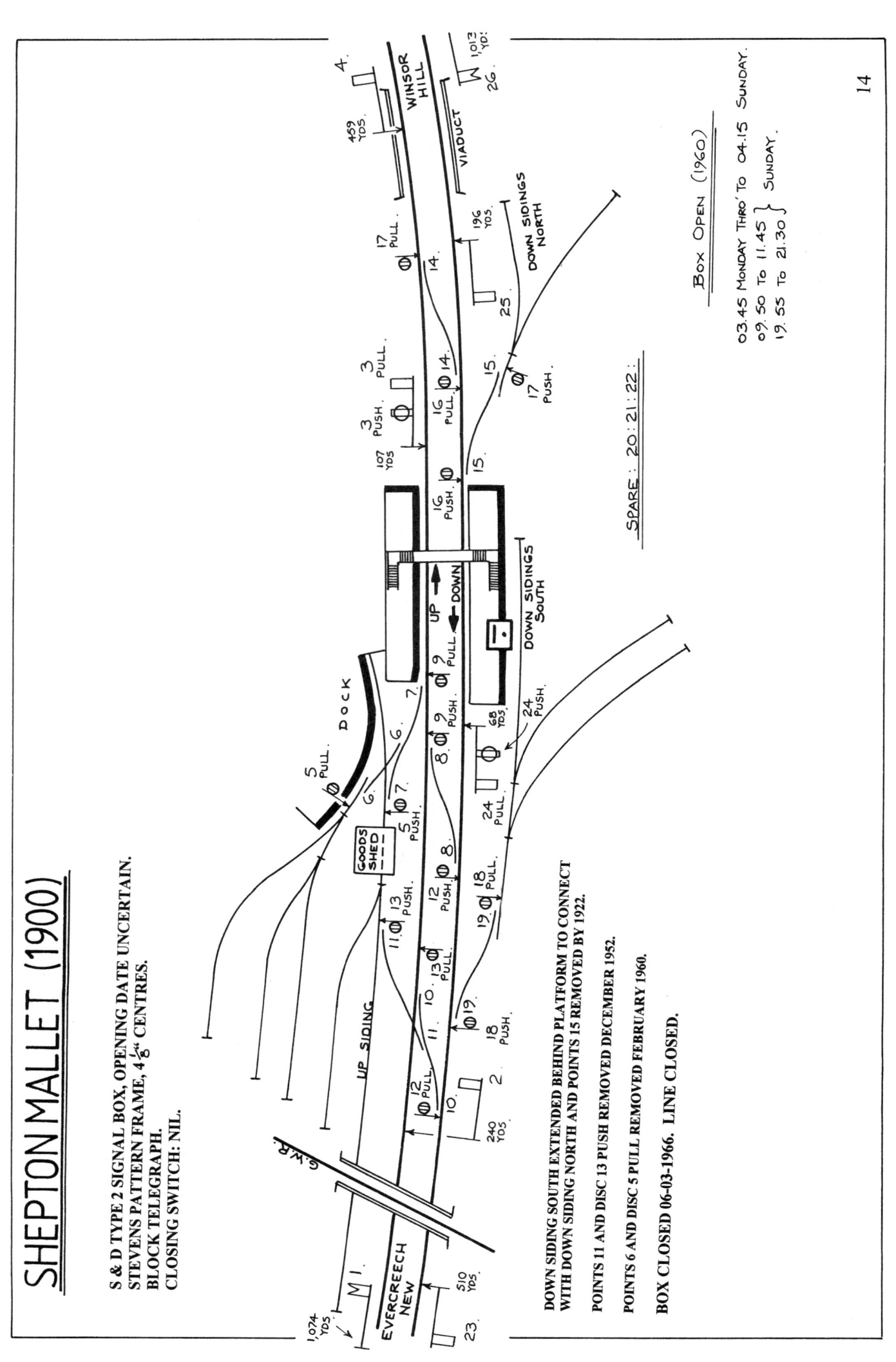

EVERCREECH NEW

L & SWR TYPE 4-STYLE BOX, OPENED 11-01-1920
TO REPLACE BOX DESTROYED BY FIRE.
TYPE OF FRAME UNCONFIRMED.
BLOCK TELEGRAPH.
CLOSING SWITCH:- ONE.

BOX CLOSED 11-10-1964.

BOX OPEN (1960)
07.15 TO 21.45 (MON. TO SAT.)
CLOSED SUNDAY.

SPARE : 4 : 14 : 17 :

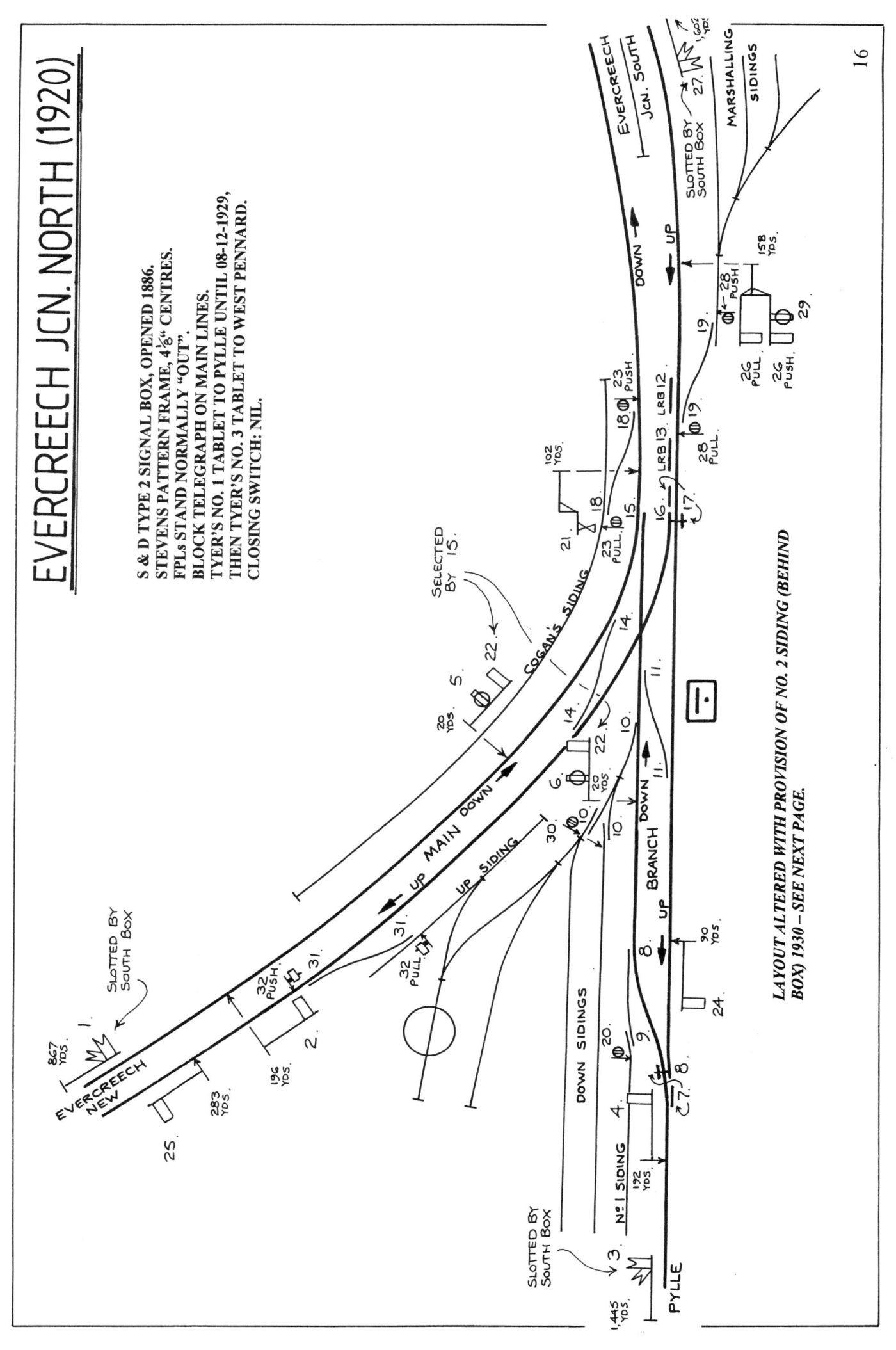

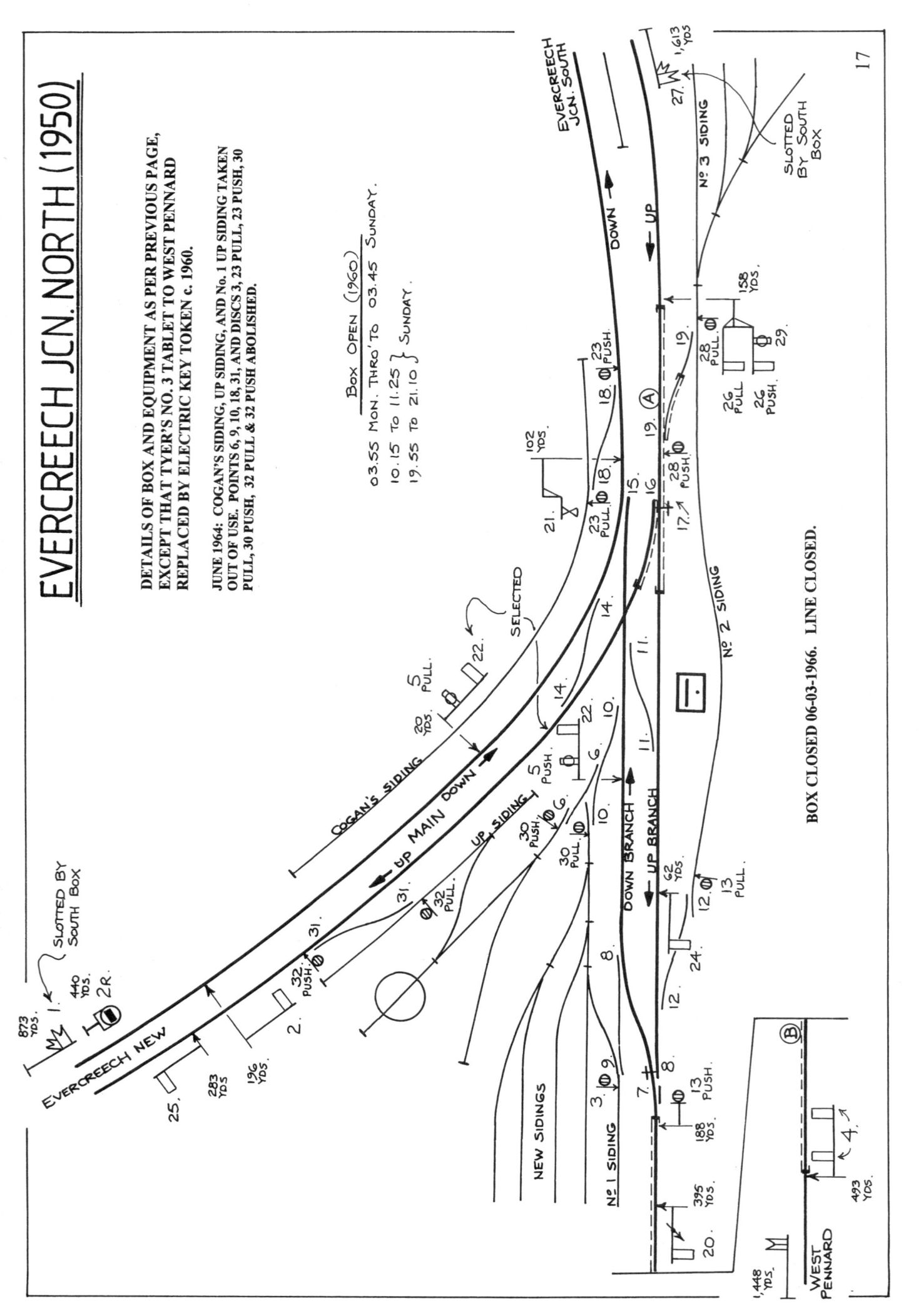

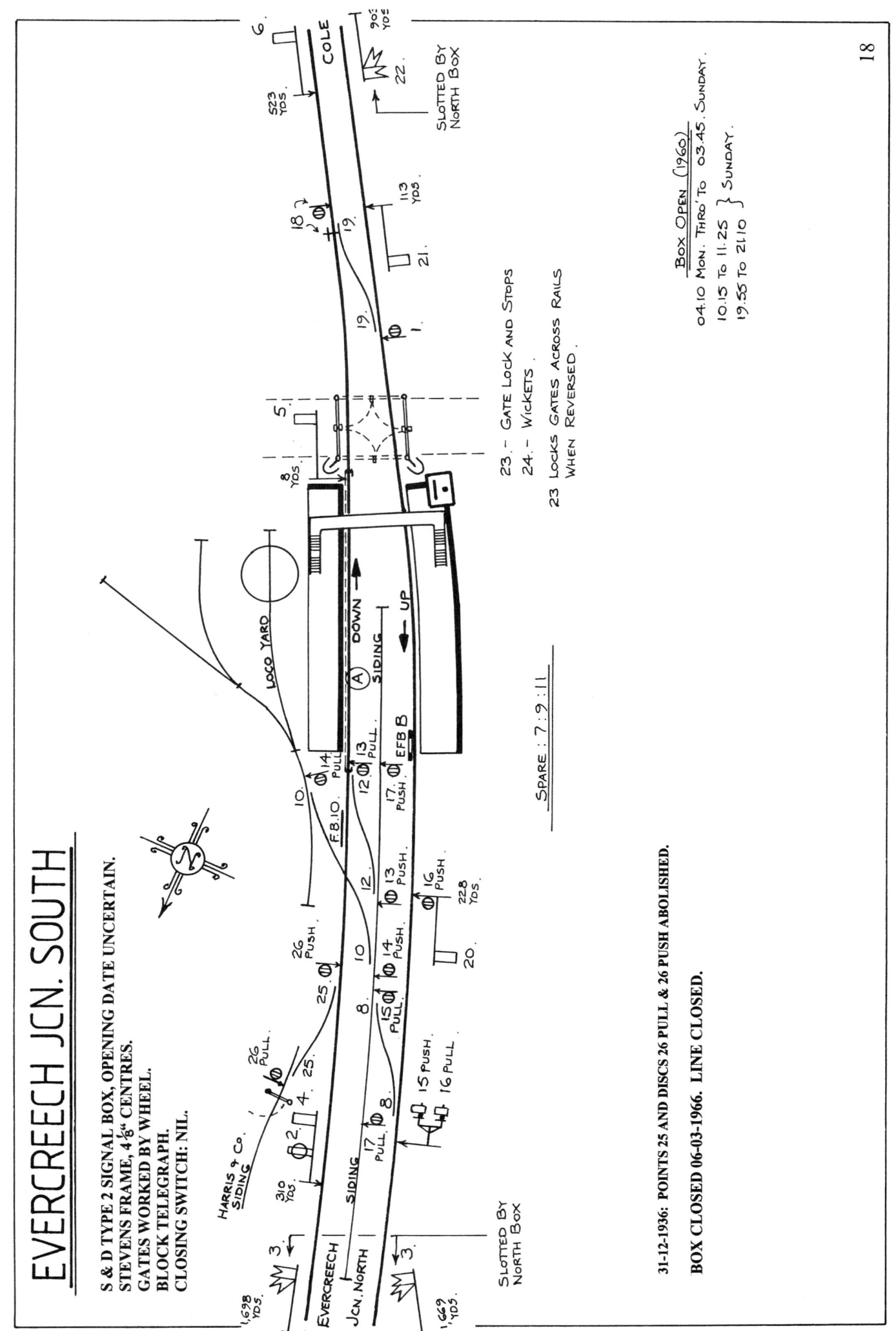

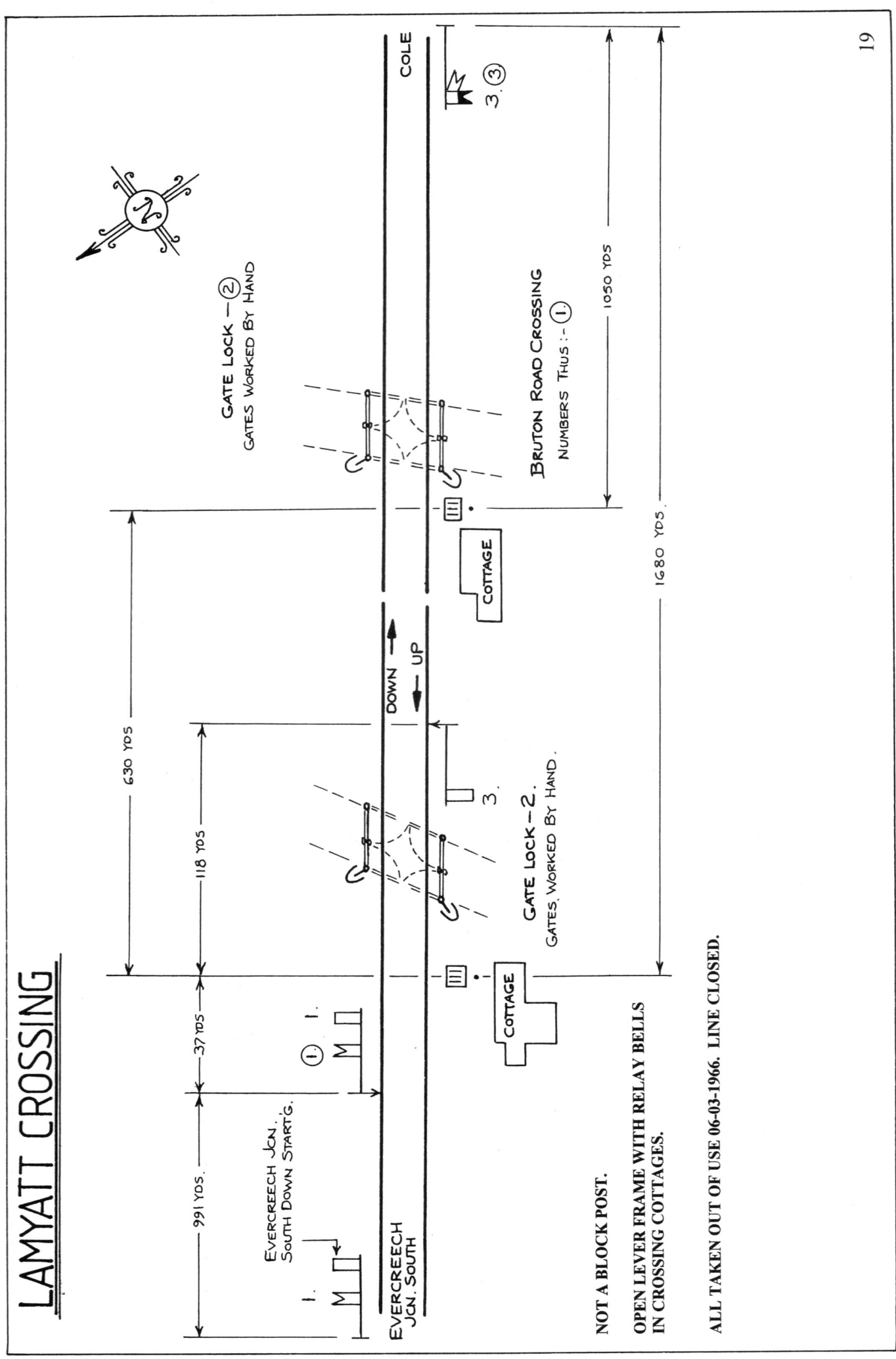

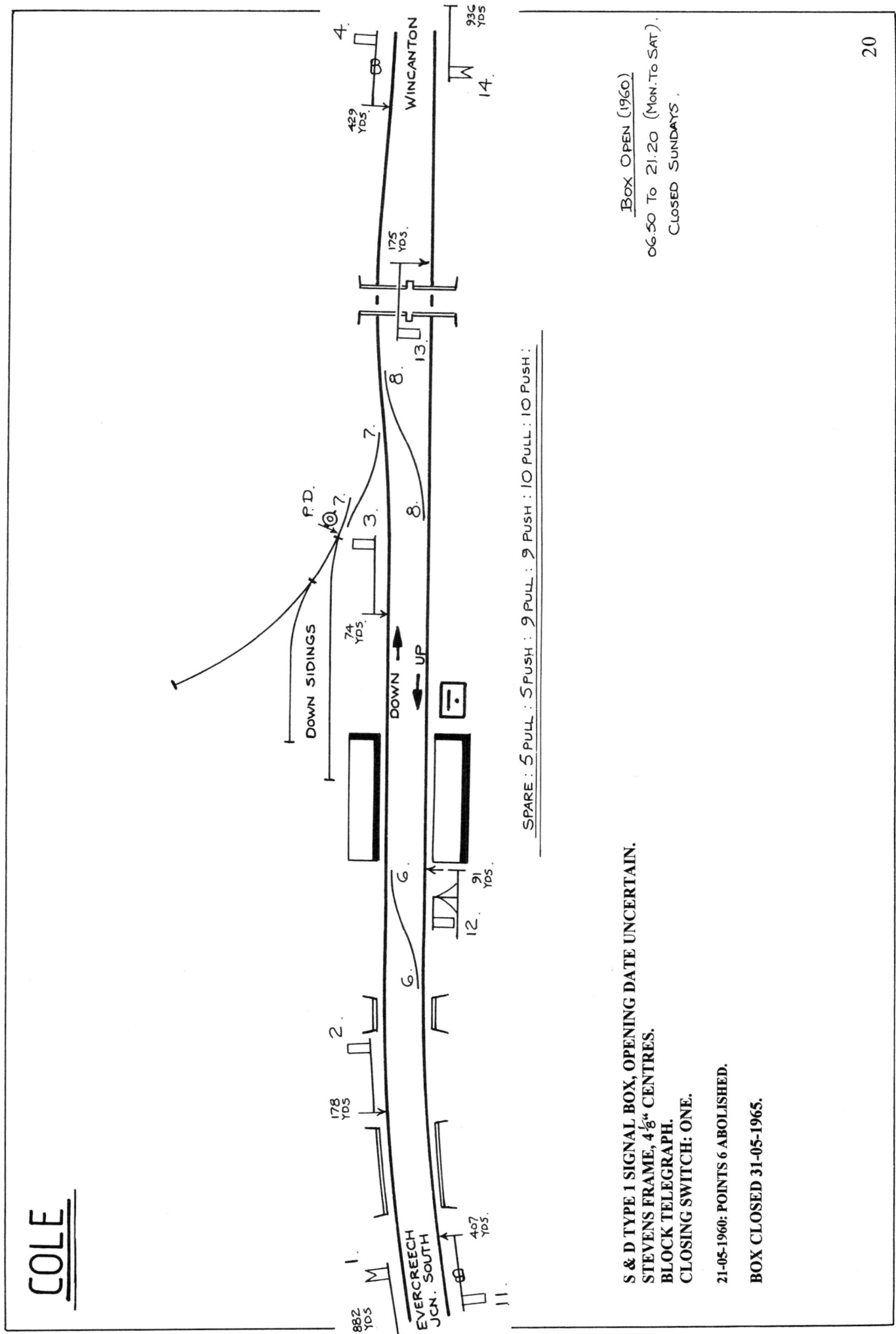

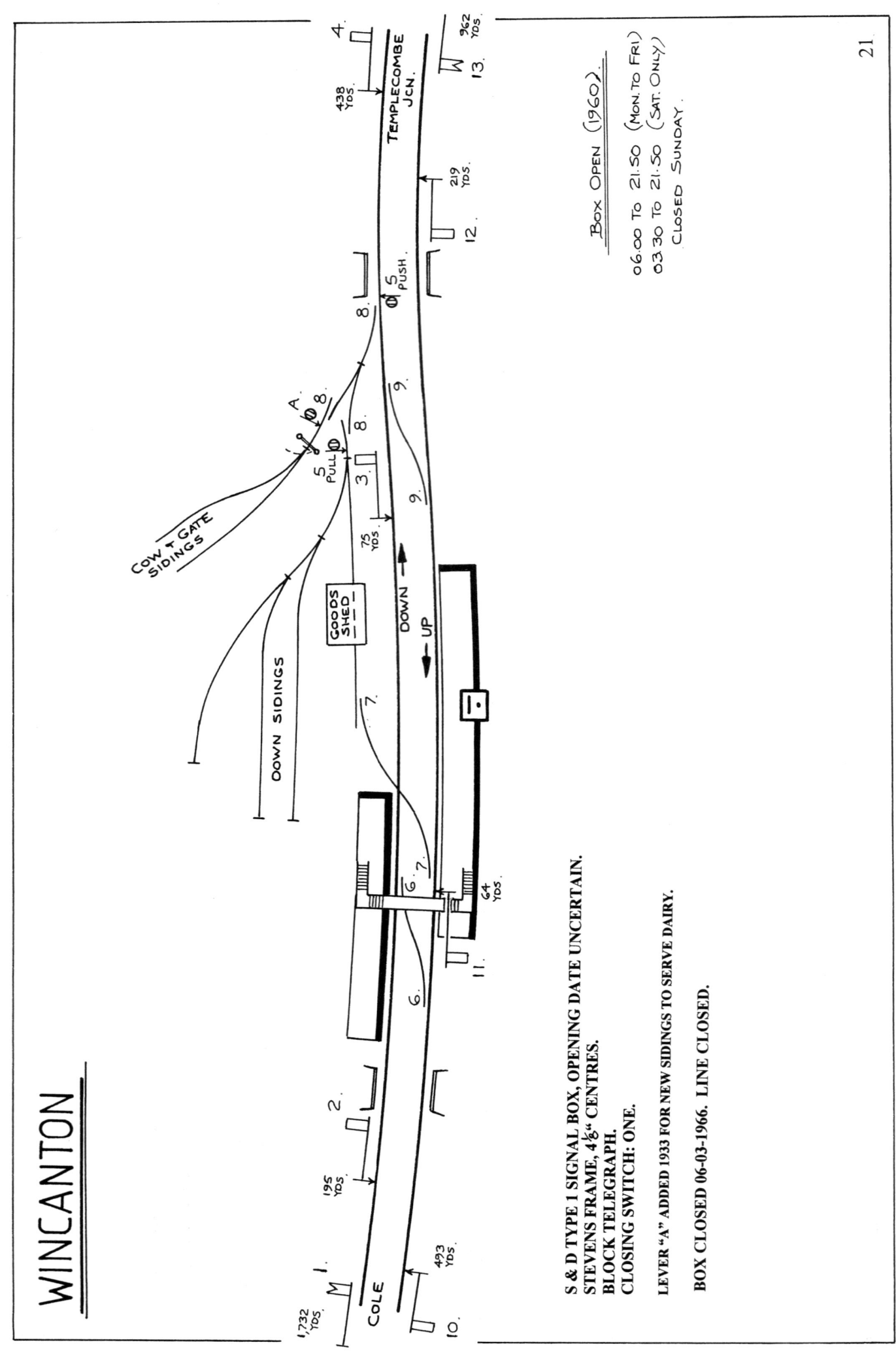

TEMPLECOMBE No 3 JCN.

SPARE :- 16.

No 14 Points Fitted with Black's Economic Lock.

SIGNAL BOX OF UNCONFIRMED TYPE OPENED
16-02-1902 TO REPLACE ORIGINAL.
STEVENS PATTERN FRAME, 4⅞" CENTRES.
FPL 11 STANDS NORMALLY "OUT".
POINTS 14 INCORPORATE "ECONOMIC" FPL AND
STAND NORMALLY BOLTED.
GATES WORKED BY WHEEL.
BLOCK TELEGRAPH ON MAIN LINES.
BELL BLOCK ON GOODS LINES.
CLOSING SWITCH :- NIL.

BOX CLOSED 12-02-1933 AND AREA TAKEN OVER
BY TEMPLECOMBE No.2 JUNCTION BOX.

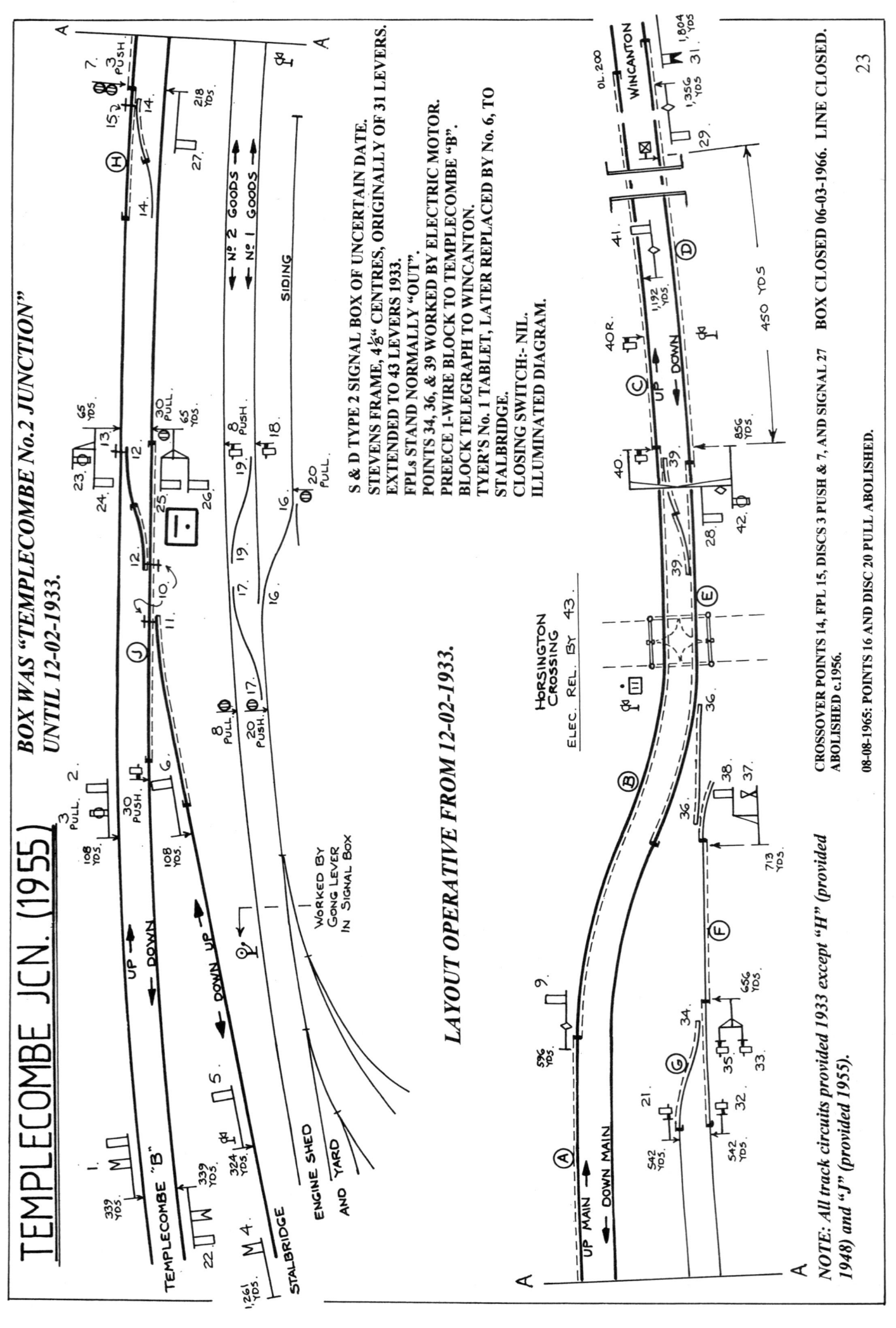

TEMPLECOMBE 'B' (1930)

S & D TYPE 1 SIGNAL BOX, ORIGINALLY WORKED
AS GROUND FRAME. UP-GRADED TO BLOCK POST
24-01-1897.
STEVENS FRAME, 4⅛" CENTRES.
PREECE 1-WIRE OPEN BLOCK.
CLOSING SWITCH:- ONE.

BOX CLOSED 07-05-1933 AND AREA TAKEN OVER BY
NEW SR BOX AT TEMPLECOMBE.

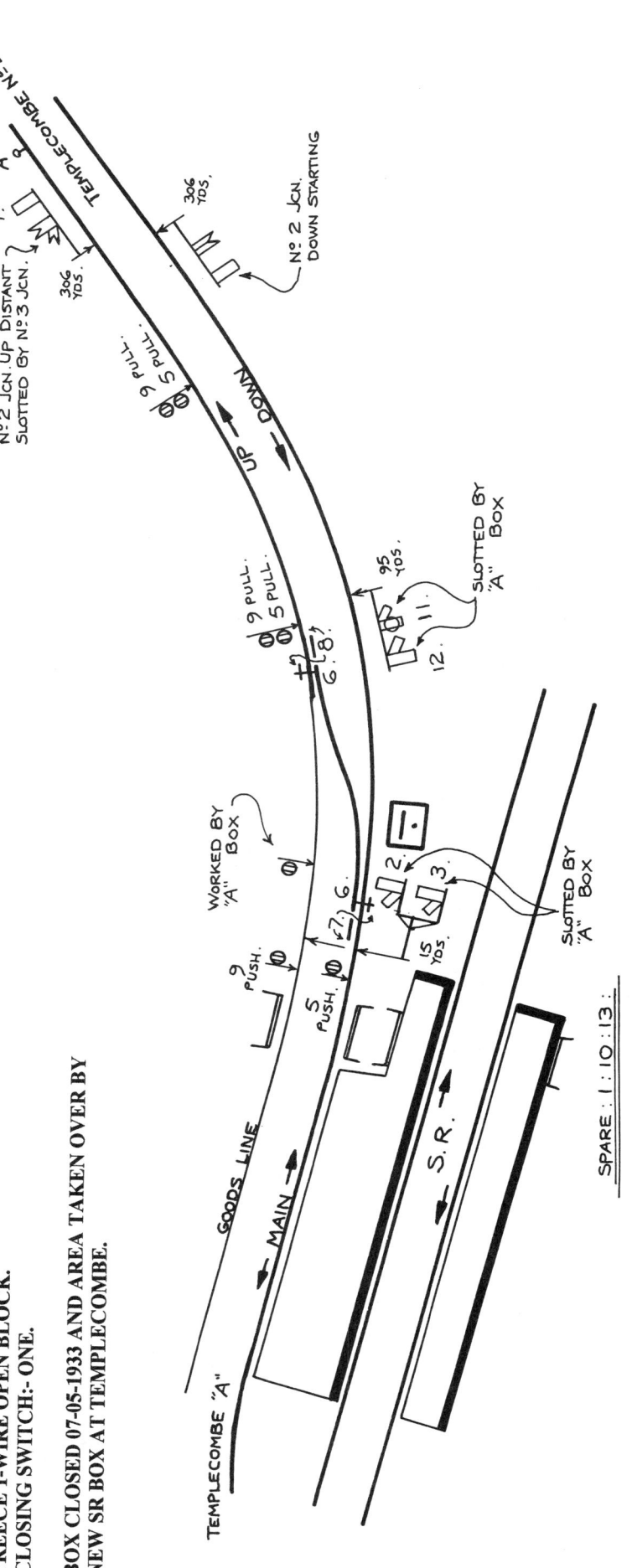

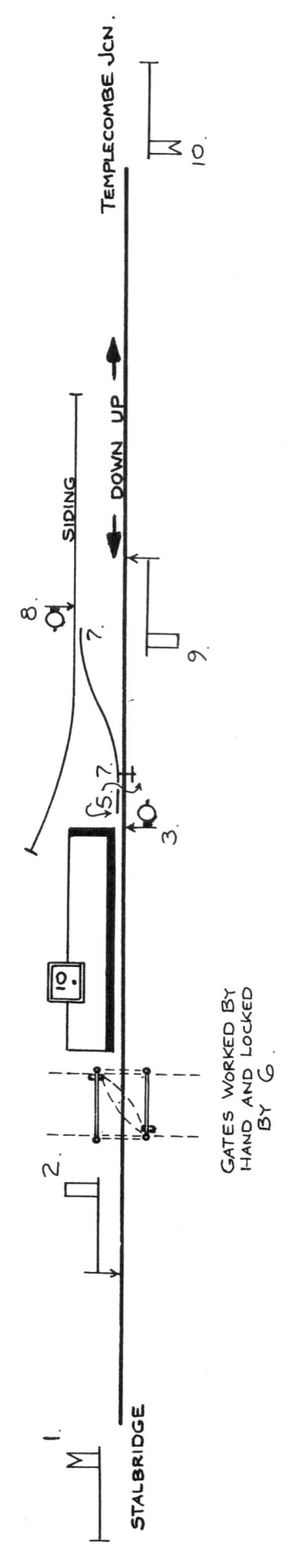

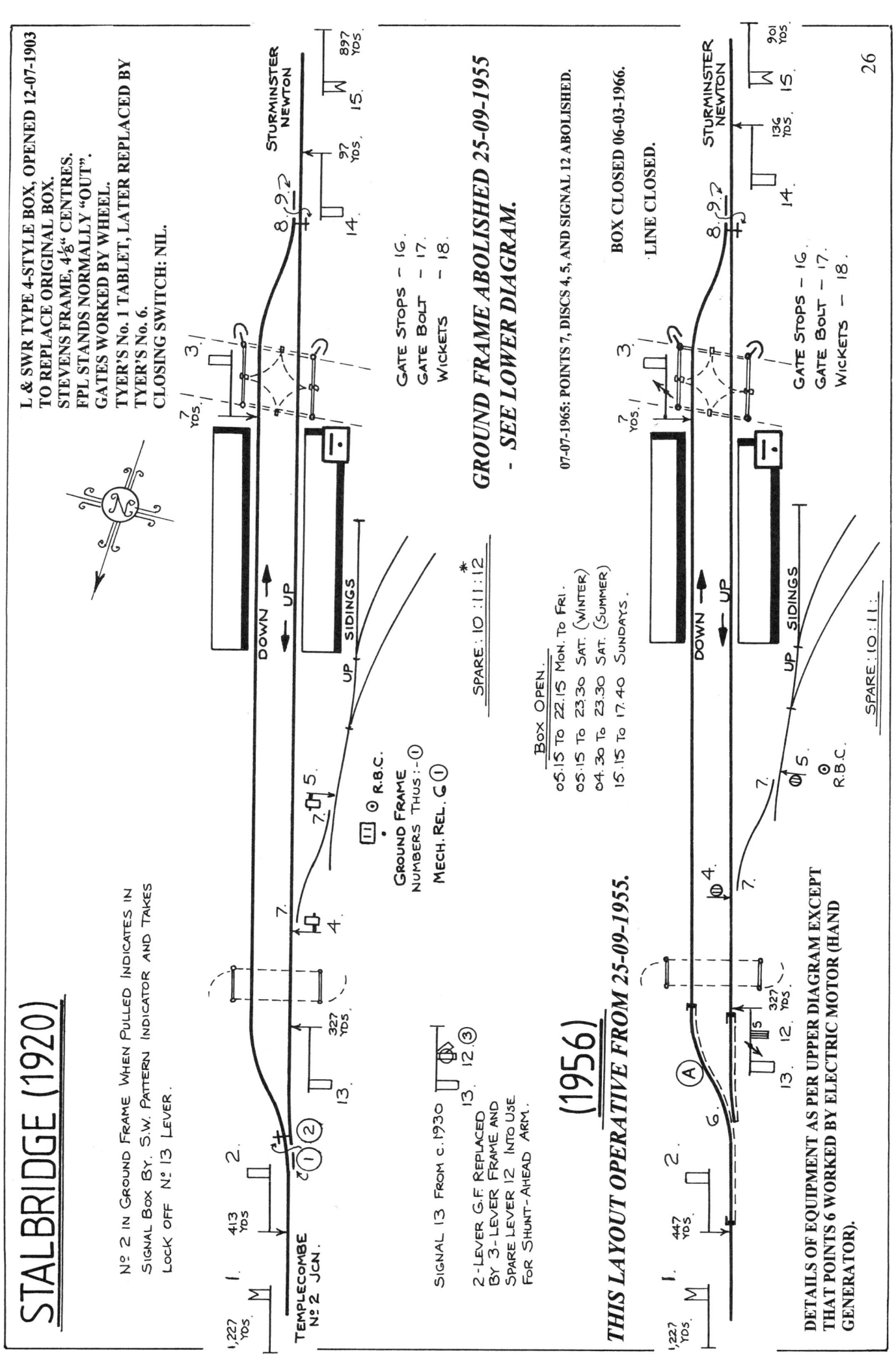

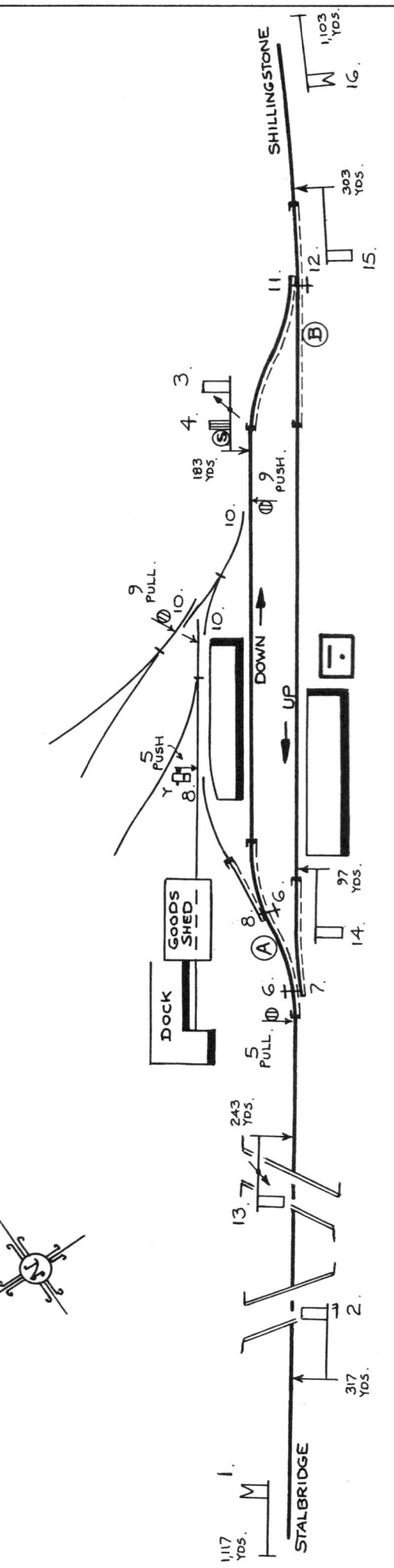

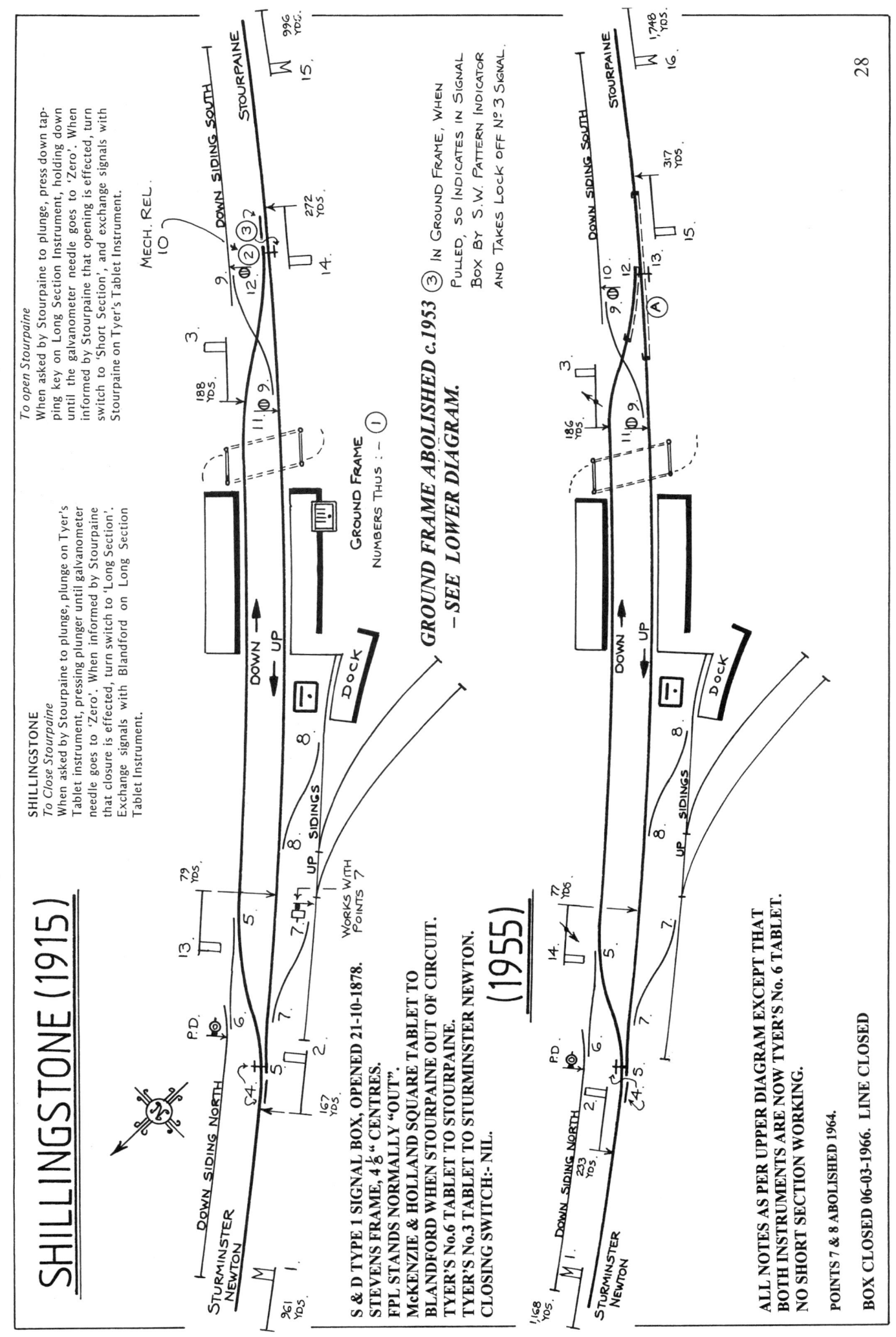

STOURPAINE

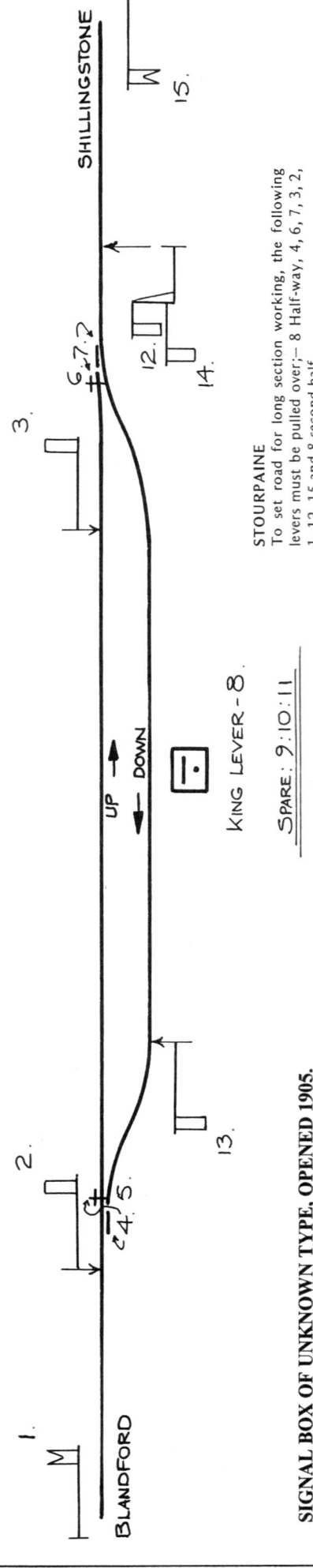

**SIGNAL BOX OF UNKNOWN TYPE, OPENED 1905.
(INSPECTED 04-07-1905).
TYPE OF FRAME UNCONFIRMED.
McKENZIE & HOLLAND SQUARE TABLET FOR LONG
SECTION WORKING SHILLINGSTONE – BLANDFORD.
TYER's No. 6 TABLET TO BLANDFORD AND SHILLINGSTONE
FOR SHORT SECTION WORKING.
CLOSING SWITCH:- ONE**

**BOX CLOSED 21-09-1925, BUT SUBSEQUENTLY REOPENED.
FINALLY CLOSED 18-12-1951.**

*NOTE: WHEN BOX OUT OF CIRCUIT ALL TRAFFIC PASSES
OVER UP LINE.*

STOURPAINE

To set road for long section working, the following levers must be pulled over:– 8 Half-way, 4, 6, 7, 3, 2, 1, 12, 15 and 8-second half.

To close

Ask Blandford and Shillingstone if they are ready to close section. If so, turn short key for closing. Phone Blandford and Shillingstone and ask them to plunge. When indicator shews 'Lock Off', turn key as far as possible, withdraw it, and take it to lever frame, inserting it in lock on Interlocking Lever, (No. 8), and turning it. Pull No. 8 to middle position, then pull over point and signal levers for through working. Pull Interlocking Lever No. 8 right over, and withdraw long key. Put key in 'Long Section' and turn as far as possible. Phone to Blandford and Shillingstone that closure is effected, and tell them to turn their switches to 'Long Section'.

To open

Ask Blandford and Shillingstone if they are ready to open section. If so, turn long key for opening. Phone Blandford and Shillingstone, and ask them to plunge. When Indicator shews 'Lock Off' turn switch as far as possible and withdraw key. Take key to lever frame and insert it in lock on Interlocking Lever No. 8, and turn it. Push No. 8 to the middle position, then return all points and signals to normal. Return Interlocking Lever No. 8 to normal, and withdraw short key. Put key in 'Short Section', and turn as far as possible. Phone to Blandford and Shillingstone that opening is effected, and tell them to turn their switches to 'Short Section'. Exchange signals with Blandford and Shillingstone on Tyer's Tablet Instruments.

BLANDFORD (1919)

"BLANDFORD FORUM" FROM 21-09-1953.

NON-STANDARD SIGNAL BOX, ERECTED 1893 BUT REBUILT AFTER FIRE DAMAGE IN 1906.
STEVENS FRAME, 4'8¼" CENTRES.
FPL 21 STANDS NORMALLY "OUT".
BLOCK TELEGRAPH TO BAILEY GATE.
McKENZIE & HOLLAND SQUARE TABLET TO SHILLINGSTONE WHEN STOURPAINE OUT OF CIRCUIT AND TYER'S No. 6 TABLET TO STOURPAINE (SHORT SECTION).
WOODEN TRAIN STAFF TO CAMP.
CLOSING SWITCH:- NIL.

1928: GROUND FRAME AND ALL SIGNALLING RELATING TO CAMP BRANCH REMOVED.

18-12-1951: McKENZIE & HOLLAND TABLET INSTRUMENT RECOVERED AND TYER'S No. 6 INSTRUMENT NOW WORKS WITH SHILLINGSTONE.

BLANDFORD
To Close Stourpaine
When asked by Stourpaine to plunge, plunge on Tyer's Tablet Instrument, pressing plunger until galvanometer needle goes to 'Zero'. When informed by Stourpaine that closing is effected, turn switch to 'Long Section'. Exchange signals with Shillingstone on long section Tablet Instrument.

To Open Stourpaine
When asked by Stourpaine to plunge, press down tapping key on Long Section Tablet Instrument, holding down until galvanometer needle goes to 'Zero'. When informed by Stourpaine that opening is effected, turn switch to 'Short Section'. Exchange signals with Stourpaine on Tyer's Tablet Instrument.

NOTE: DOUBLE LINE TO BAILEY GATE INTO USE 29-04-1901. CAMP BRANCH INTO USE 1919 AND CLOSED 1928.

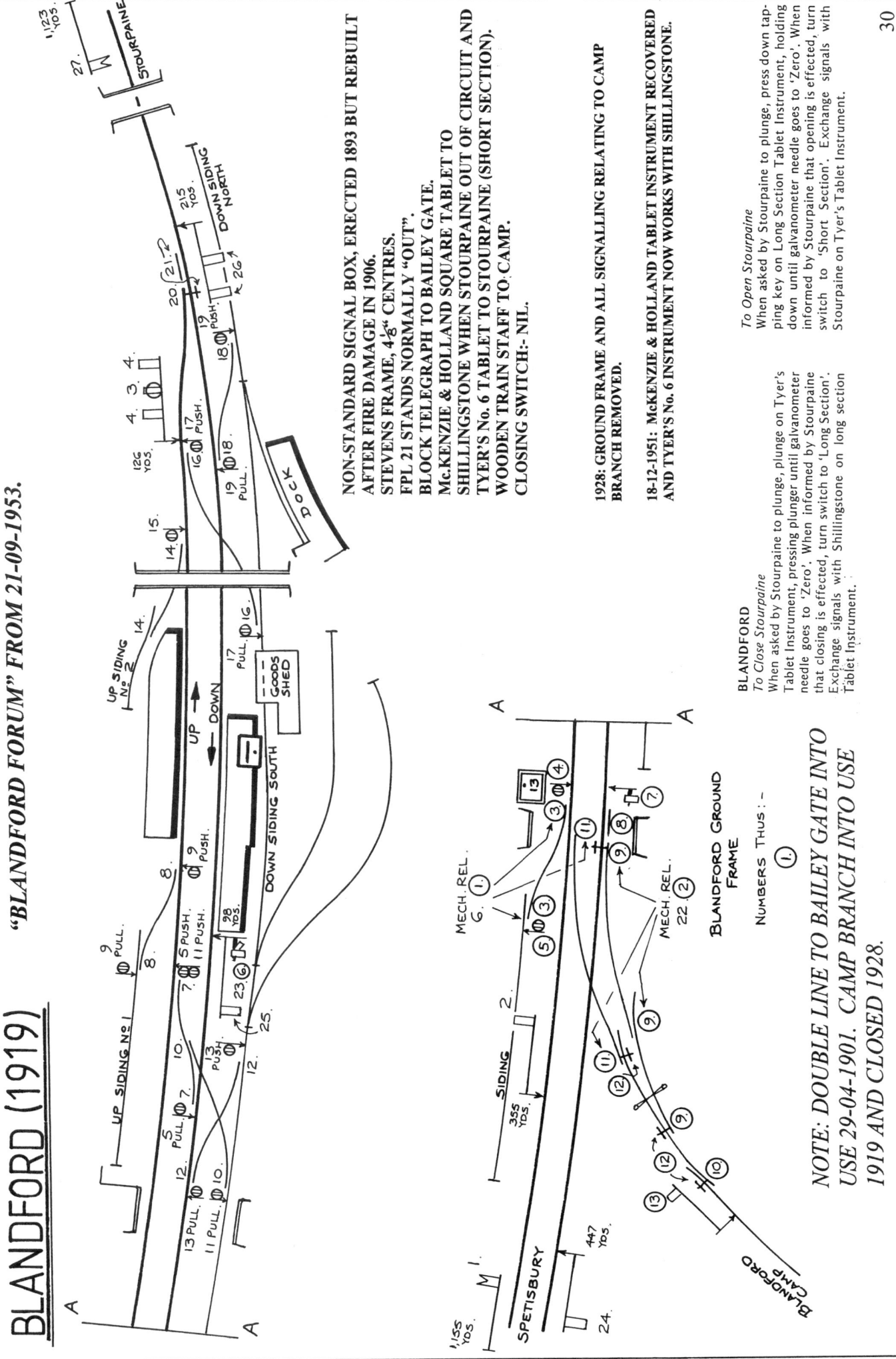

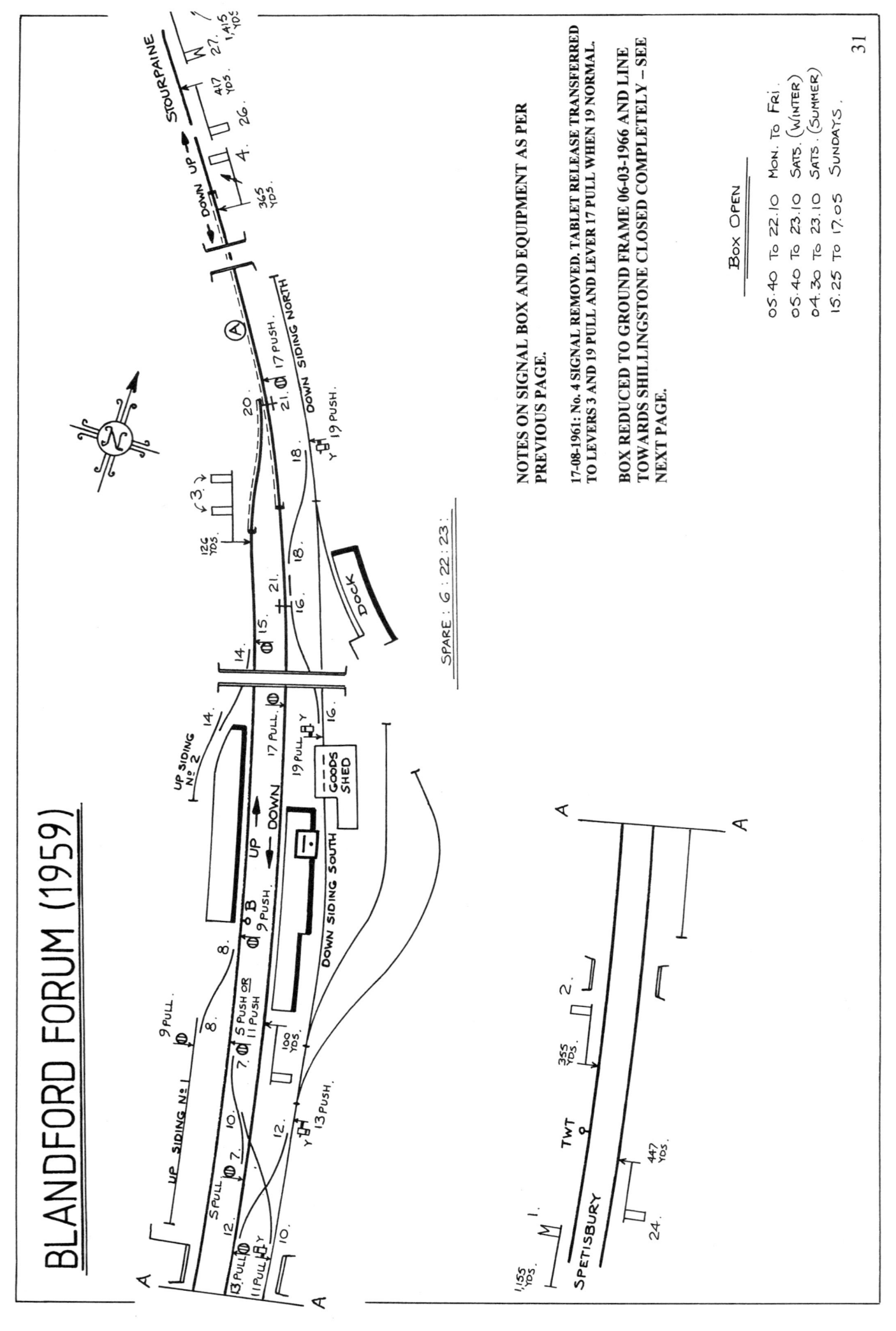

BLANDFORD FORUM (1967)

THIS ARRANGEMENT APPLIED FROM
06-03-1966.

* Board worded "Stop. Do Not Proceed Without Shunter's Permission".

SPARE : 1 : 2 : 3 : 4 : 5 : 6 : 8 : 9 : 10 : 11 : 13 : 14 : 15 : 17 : 18 : 19 : 21 : 22 : 23 : 24 : 25 : 26 : 27 :

NOT A BLOCK POST: WORKED AS GROUND FRAME.

BOX ABOLISHED 07-05-1968 AND POINTS CONVERTED TO HAND OPERATION.

SPETISBURY

GROUND-LEVEL SIGNAL BOX OPENED 1901.
TYPE OF LEVER FRAME UNKNOWN.
BLOCK TELEGRAPH.
CLOSING SWITCH: ONE.

BOX CLOSED 10-08-1952.

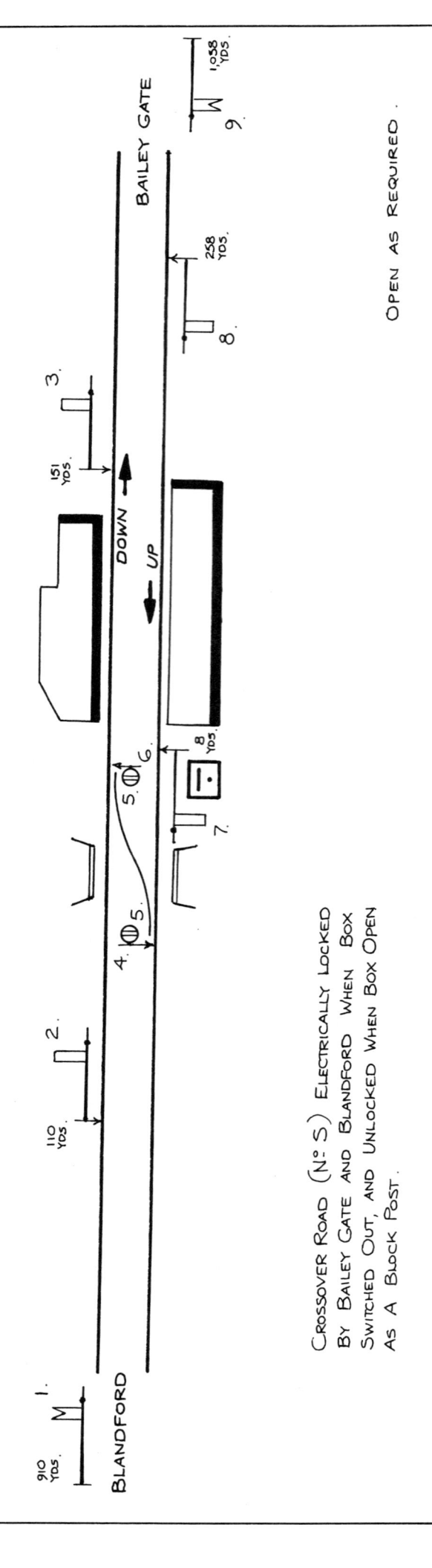

Crossover Road (Nº 5) Electrically Locked By Bailey Gate And Blandford When Box Switched Out, And Unlocked When Box Open As A Block Post.

Open As Required.

BAILEY GATE (1904)

THIS ARRANGEMENT APPLIED FROM 29-04-1901, WHEN LINE DOUBLED TO BLANDFORD.

S & D TYPE 1 SIGNAL BOX, OPENED 10-02-1879.
STEVENS FRAME, 4⅛" CENTRES.
FPLs STAND NORMALLY "OUT".
BLOCK TELEGRAPH TO SPETISBURY.
TYER'S TABLETS (TYPES UNCONFIRMED) TO WIMBORNE JCN. AND BROADSTONE.
CLOSING SWITCH:- NIL.

16-04-1905: PARALLEL SINGLE LINES CONVERTED INTO UP AND DOWN LINES TO NEW SIGNAL BOX AT CORFE MULLEN. TABLET INSTRUMENTS REMOVED AND REPLACED BY MIDLAND-PATTERN BLOCK TELEGRAPH. CLOSING SWITCH PROVIDED. DOWN RUNNING SIGNALS ALTERED (SEE NEXT PAGE) AND LEVERS 5, 6, 7, & 8 MADE SPARE. SIGNALS 17 AND 18 REMOVED, BUT LEVERS REUSED FOR UP HOME AND UP DISTANT MAKING 19 AND 20 SPARE. POINTS 12 AND FPLs 13 AND 14 ABOLISHED.

BAILEY GATE (1920)

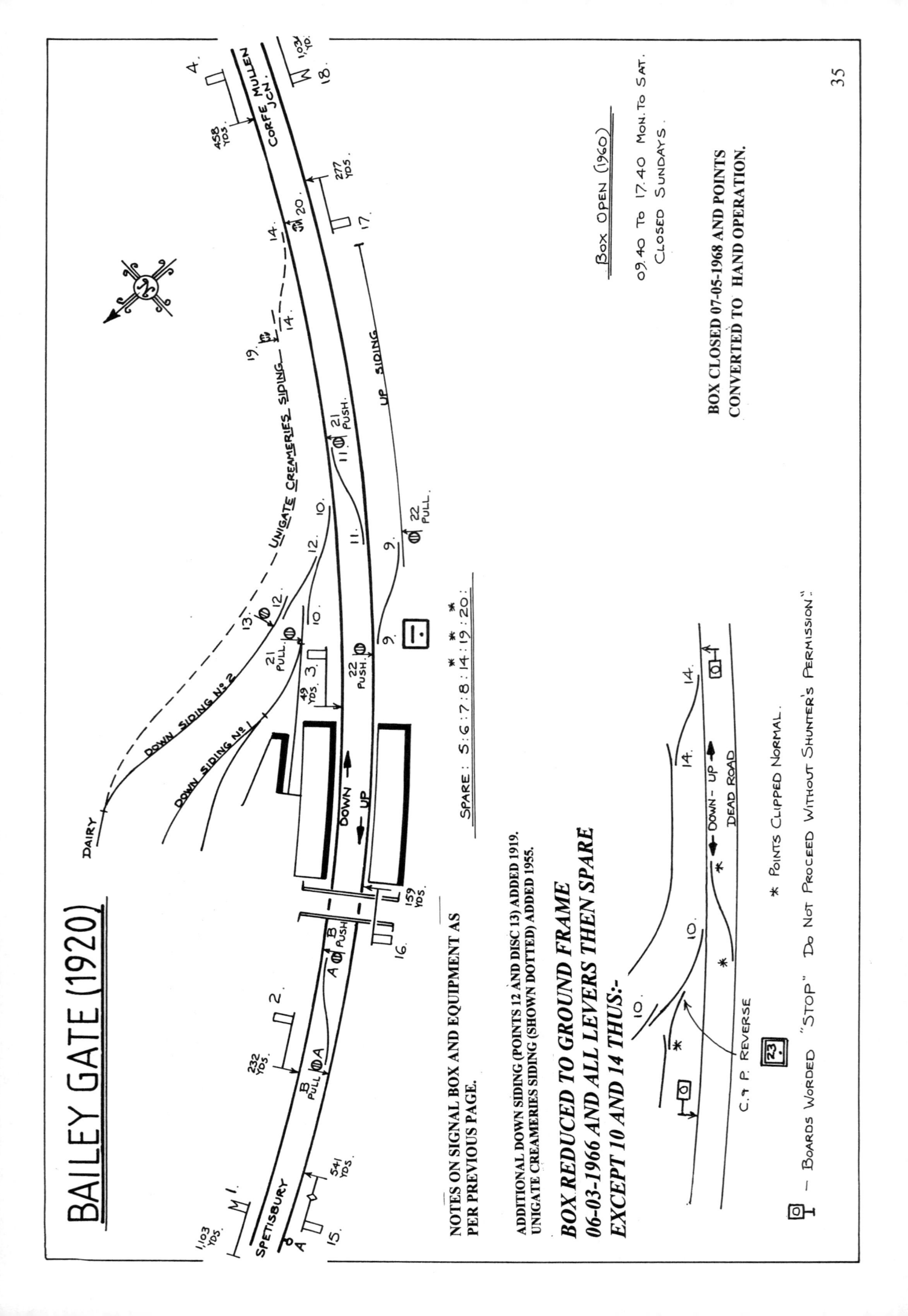

NOTES ON SIGNAL BOX AND EQUIPMENT AS PER PREVIOUS PAGE.

ADDITIONAL DOWN SIDING (POINTS 12 AND DISC 13) ADDED 1919.
UNIGATE CREAMERIES SIDING (SHOWN DOTTED) ADDED 1955.

BOX REDUCED TO GROUND FRAME 06-03-1966 AND ALL LEVERS THEN SPARE EXCEPT 10 AND 14 THUS:-

SPARE : 5 ; 6 ; 7 ; 8 ; 14 ; 19 ; 20 ;

* — Points Clipped Normal.

* — Boards Worded "Stop" Do Not Proceed Without Shunter's Permission.

Box Open (1960)

09.40 to 17.40 Mon. to Sat.
Closed Sundays.

BOX CLOSED 07-05-1968 AND POINTS CONVERTED TO HAND OPERATION.

35

BAILEY GATE CROSSING (1915)

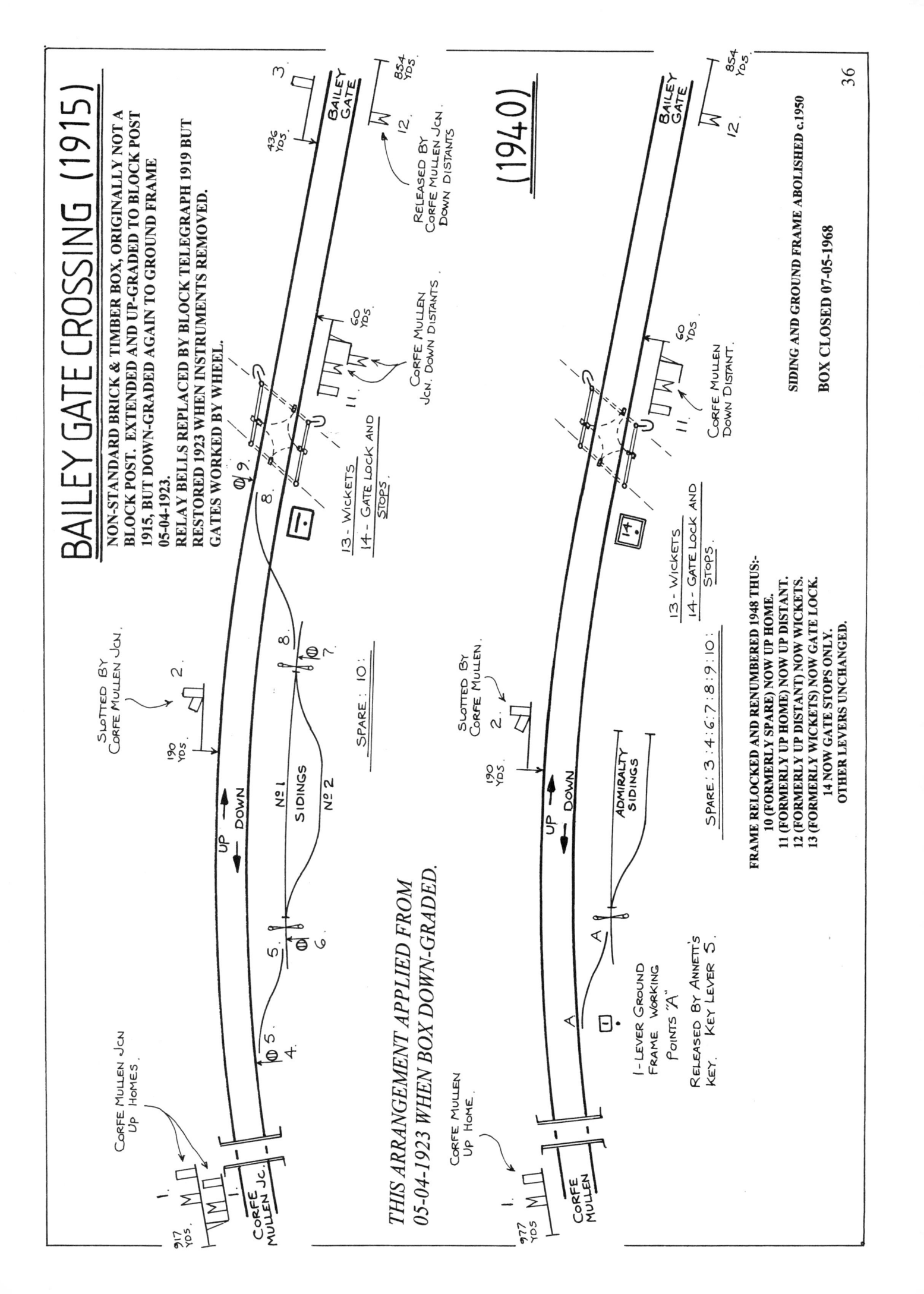

NON-STANDARD BRICK & TIMBER BOX, ORIGINALLY NOT A BLOCK POST. EXTENDED AND UP-GRADED TO BLOCK POST 1915, BUT DOWN-GRADED AGAIN TO GROUND FRAME 05-04-1923.
RELAY BELLS REPLACED BY BLOCK TELEGRAPH 1919 BUT RESTORED 1923 WHEN INSTRUMENTS REMOVED. GATES WORKED BY WHEEL.

- Corfe Mullen Jcn Up Homes.
- Slotted by Corfe Mullen Jcn.
- Released by Corfe Mullen Jcn Down Distants
- 13 - Wickets
- 14 - Gate lock and stops.
- SPARE : 10.

THIS ARRANGEMENT APPLIED FROM 05-04-1923 WHEN BOX DOWN-GRADED.

(1940)

- Corfe Mullen Up Home.
- Slotted by Corfe Mullen.
- 1-Lever Ground Frame working Points "A". Released by Annett's key. Key Lever 5.
- Admiralty Sidings
- Corfe Mullen Down Distant.
- 13 - Wickets
- 14 - Gate lock and stops.

FRAME RELOCKED AND RENUMBERED 1948 THUS:-
10 (FORMERLY SPARE) NOW UP HOME.
11 (FORMERLY UP HOME) NOW UP DISTANT.
12 (FORMERLY UP DISTANT) NOW WICKETS.
13 (FORMERLY WICKETS) NOW GATE LOCK.
14 NOW GATE STOPS ONLY.
OTHER LEVERS UNCHANGED.

SPARE : 3 : 4 : 6 : 7 : 8 : 9 : 10.

SIDING AND GROUND FRAME ABOLISHED c.1950

BOX CLOSED 07-05-1968

CORFE MULLEN JCN. (1905)

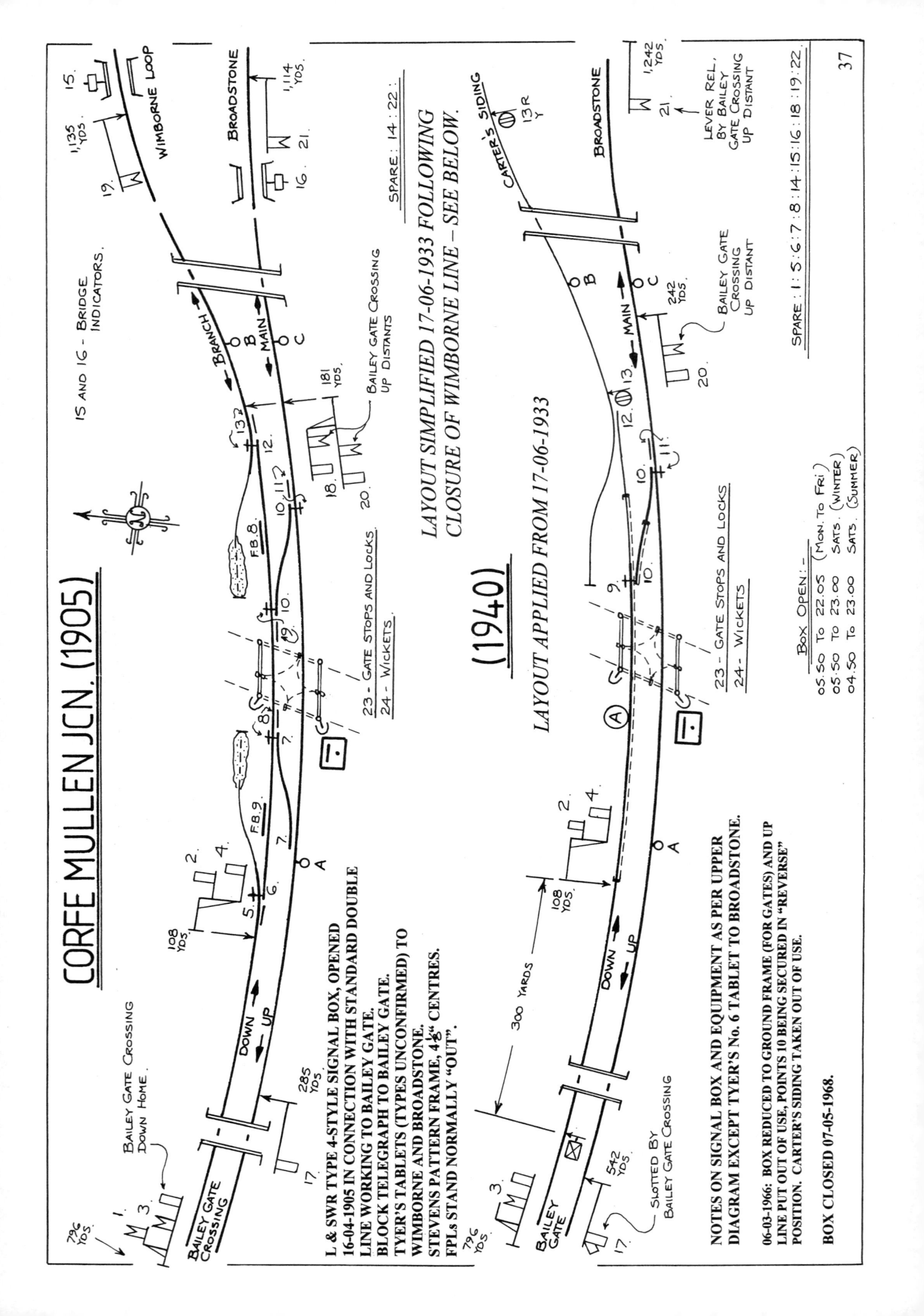

Bailey Gate Crossing Down Home.
796 YDS.
1, 3 M
Bailey Gate Crossing
17
285 YDS.
DOWN
UP
108 YDS.
5, 6
2, 4
F.B. 9
7
A
8
10
9
F.B. 8
12
13
181 YDS.
18 W W — Bailey Gate Crossing Up Distants
20
15 and 16 - Bridge Indicators.
1,135 YDS.
19 W — Wimborne Loop
15
BRANCH
MAIN
B
C
1,114 YDS.
16, 21 M — Broadstone

23 - Gate Stops and Locks
24 - Wickets
SPARE : 14 : 22 :

L. & S.W.R TYPE 4-STYLE SIGNAL BOX, OPENED 16-04-1905 IN CONNECTION WITH STANDARD DOUBLE LINE WORKING TO BAILEY GATE.
BLOCK TELEGRAPH TO BAILEY GATE.
TYER'S TABLETS (TYPES UNCONFIRMED) TO WIMBORNE AND BROADSTONE.
STEVENS PATTERN FRAME, 4¾" CENTRES.
FPLs STAND NORMALLY "OUT".

LAYOUT SIMPLIFIED 17-06-1933 FOLLOWING CLOSURE OF WIMBORNE LINE – SEE BELOW.

(1940)

LAYOUT APPLIED FROM 17-06-1933

Bailey Gate
796 YDS.
3 M
Slotted by Bailey Gate Crossing
17
542 YDS.
300 YARDS
DOWN
UP
108 YDS.
2, 4
A
9
10
11
12
13
13R Y — Carter's Siding
242 YDS.
20 W — Bailey Gate Crossing Up Distant
MAIN
B
C
1,242 YDS.
21 W — Broadstone
Lever Rel. by Bailey Gate Crossing Up Distant

23 - Gate Stops and Locks
24 - Wickets
SPARE : 1 : 5 : 6 : 7 : 8 : 14 : 15 : 16 : 18 : 19 : 22 :

NOTES ON SIGNAL BOX AND EQUIPMENT AS PER UPPER DIAGRAM EXCEPT TYER'S No. 6 TABLET TO BROADSTONE.

06-03-1966: BOX REDUCED TO GROUND FRAME (FOR GATES) AND UP LINE PUT OUT OF USE, POINTS 10 BEING SECURED IN "REVERSE" POSITION. CARTER'S SIDING TAKEN OUT OF USE.

BOX CLOSED 07-05-1968.

Box Open:-
05.50 To 22.05 (Mon. To Fri)
05.50 To 23.00 Sats. (Winter)
04.50 To 23.00 Sats. (Summer)

SECTION TWO

BURNHAM-ON-SEA TO EVERCREECH JUNCTION

OPENED

HIGHBRIDGE TO GLASTONBURY 28-08-1854

HIGHBRIDGE TO BURNHAM-ON-SEA 15-03-1859

GLASTONBURY TO EVERCREECH JCN. 03-02-1862

(Through to Templecombe)

CLOSED

HIGHBRIDGE TO BURNHAM-ON-SEA 29-10-1951 (Pass.) & 20-05-1963 (Goods)

HIGHBRIDGE TO EVERCREECH JCN. TO PASSENGERS THROUGHOUT AND TO ALL TRAFFIC BETWEEN BASON BRIDGE AND EVERCREECH JCN. 07-03-1966

(LAST TRAFFIC 06-03-66)

HIGHBRIDGE TO BASON BRIDGE 03-10-1972 (completely)

BURNHAM-ON-SEA (1915)

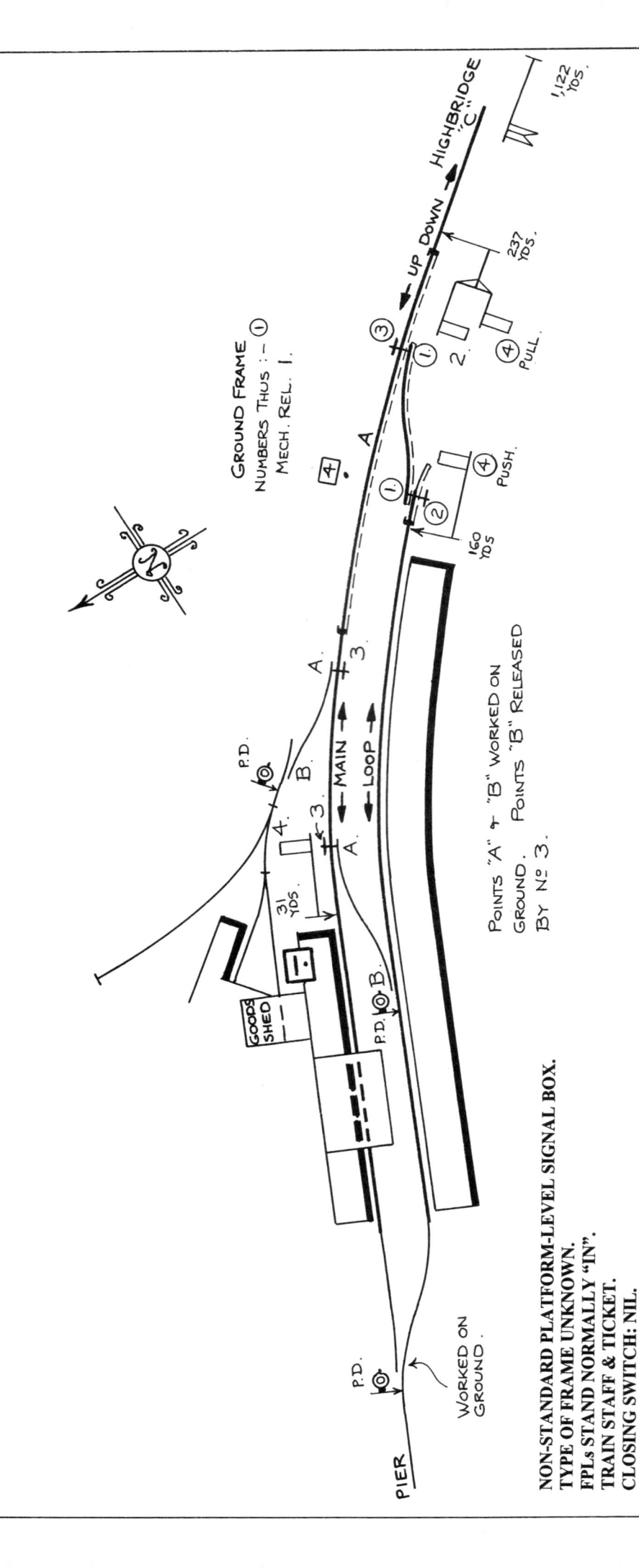

NON-STANDARD PLATFORM-LEVEL SIGNAL BOX.
TYPE OF FRAME UNKNOWN.
FPLs STAND NORMALLY "IN".
TRAIN STAFF & TICKET.
CLOSING SWITCH: NIL.

NOTE: LOCKING WAS ALTERED IN 1914. BEFORE THEN SIGNAL 2 WAS "2 PULL" AND SIGNAL 4 WAS "2 PUSH", LEVER 4 BEING SPARE.

13-04-1933: HAND POINTS FROM PIER ROAD MOVED 88 YARDS NEARER TO SIGNAL BOX AND POINT DISC RECOVERED.

BOX CLOSED 20-05-1963 AND LINE TAKEN OUT OF USE.

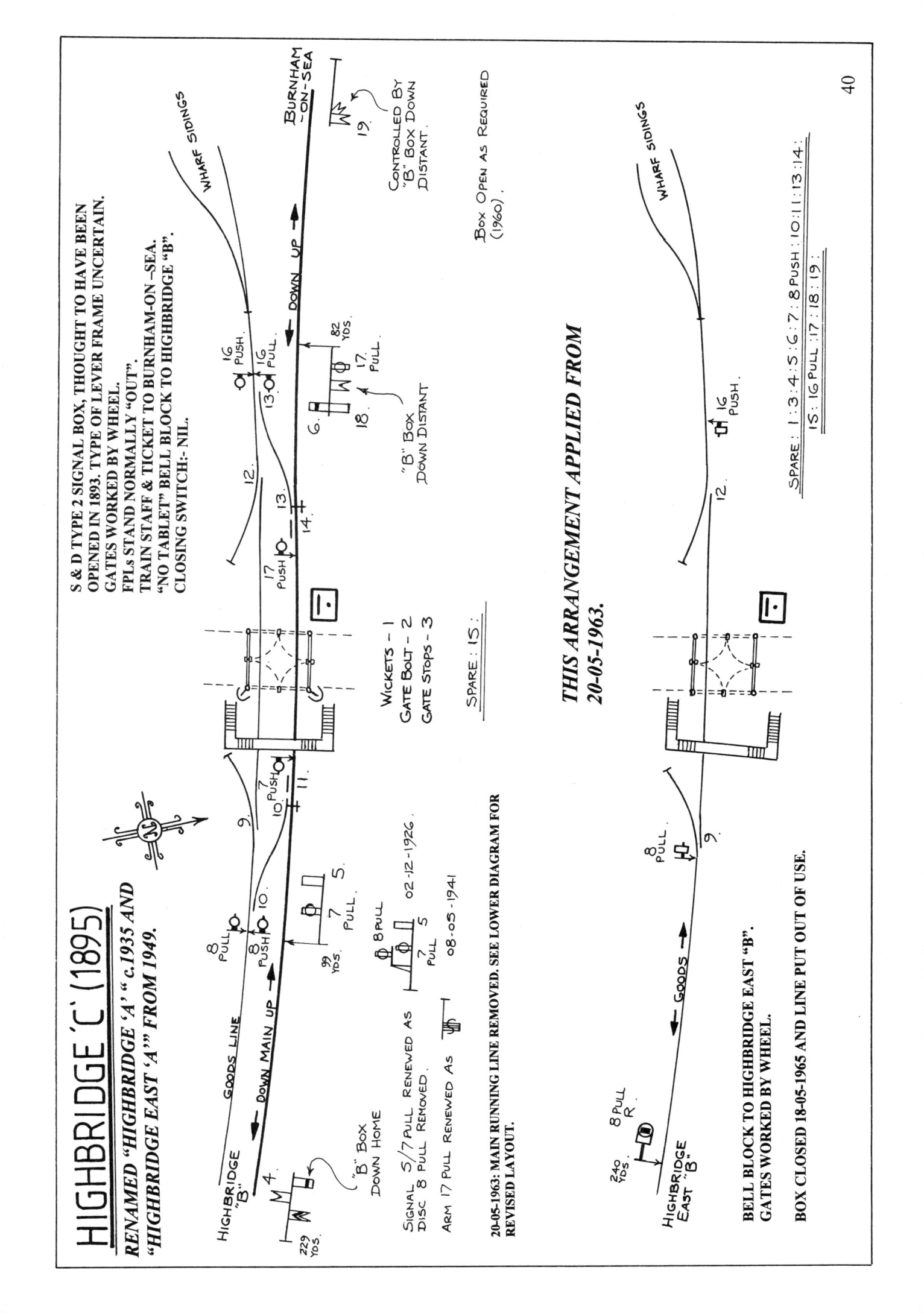

HIGHBRIDGE 'C' (1895)

RENAMED "HIGHBRIDGE 'A'" c.1935 AND "HIGHBRIDGE EAST 'A'" FROM 1949.

S & D TYPE 2 SIGNAL BOX, THOUGHT TO HAVE BEEN OPENED IN 1893. TYPE OF LEVER FRAME UNCERTAIN. GATES WORKED BY WHEEL.
FPLs STAND NORMALLY "OUT".
TRAIN STAFF & TICKET TO BURNHAM-ON-SEA.
"NO TABLET" BELL BLOCK TO HIGHBRIDGE "B".
CLOSING SWITCH:- NIL.

Wickets - 1
Gate Bolt - 2
Gate Stops - 3

SPARE : 15 :

"B" Box Down Distant

Box Open As Required (1960).

Signal 5/7 Pull Renewed As Disc 8 Pull Removed. 02-12-1926.

Arm 17 Pull Renewed As [symbol] 08-05-1941

20-05-1963: MAIN RUNNING LINE REMOVED. SEE LOWER DIAGRAM FOR REVISED LAYOUT.

THIS ARRANGEMENT APPLIED FROM 20-05-1963.

BELL BLOCK TO HIGHBRIDGE EAST "B". GATES WORKED BY WHEEL.

BOX CLOSED 18-05-1965 AND LINE PUT OUT OF USE.

SPARE : 1 : 3 : 4 : 5 : 6 : 7 : 8 PUSH : 10 : 11 : 13 : 14 :
15 : 16 PULL : 17 : 18 : 19 :

40

HIGHBRIDGE 'B'

RENAMED "HIGHBRIDGE EAST 'B'" 1949.

S & D TYPE 1 BOX ON BRICK BASE, OPENED 15-05-1877.
STEVENS FRAME, 4⅛" CENTRES.
"NO TABLET" BELL BLOCK.
CLOSING SWITCH:- NIL.

"A" BOX CLOSED 1914, AND SIGNAL SLOTS THEREAFTER WORKED ONLY FROM GWR WEST BOX.

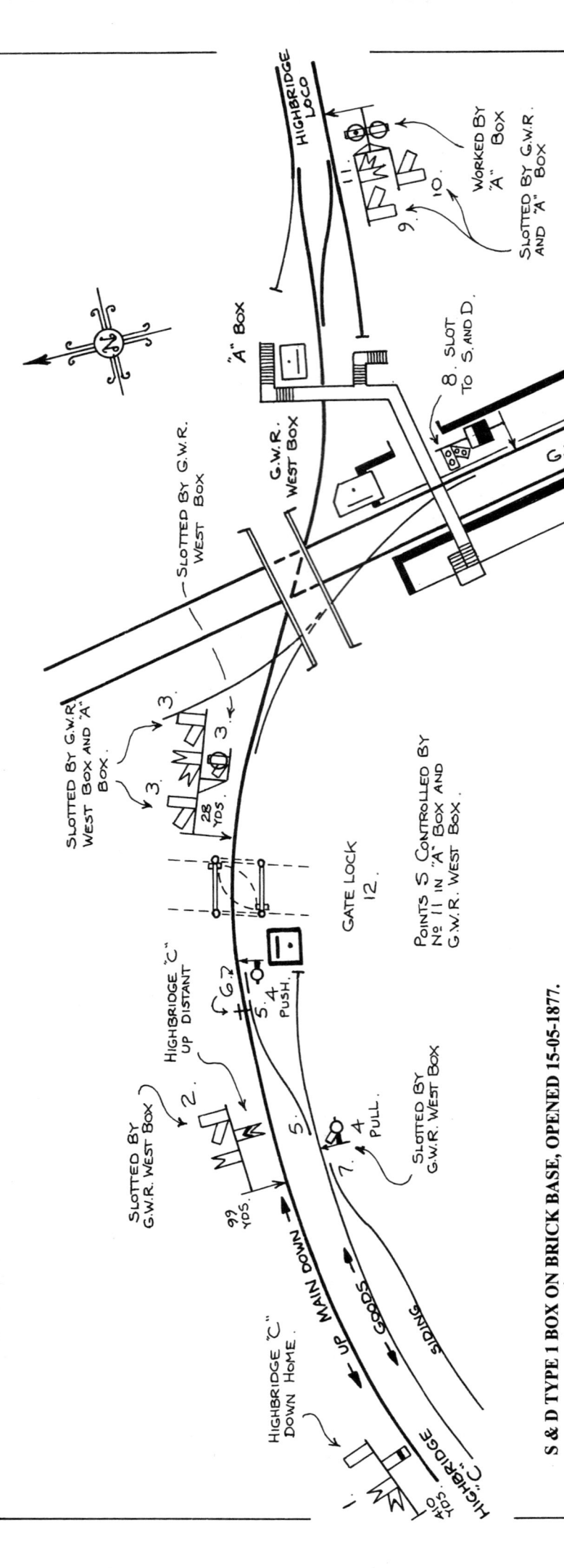

20-05-1963: MAIN RUNNING LINE REMOVED TOWARDS BURNHAM-ON-SEA AND POINTS 5 SECURED IN "REVERSE" POSITION. SIGNALS 1 AND 2 REMOVED AND SIGNAL 9 FIXED AT "DANGER".

04-03-1965: POINTS 7 TAKEN OUT OF USE.

BOX CLOSED 15-06-1965.

HIGHBRIDGE 'A' (1900)

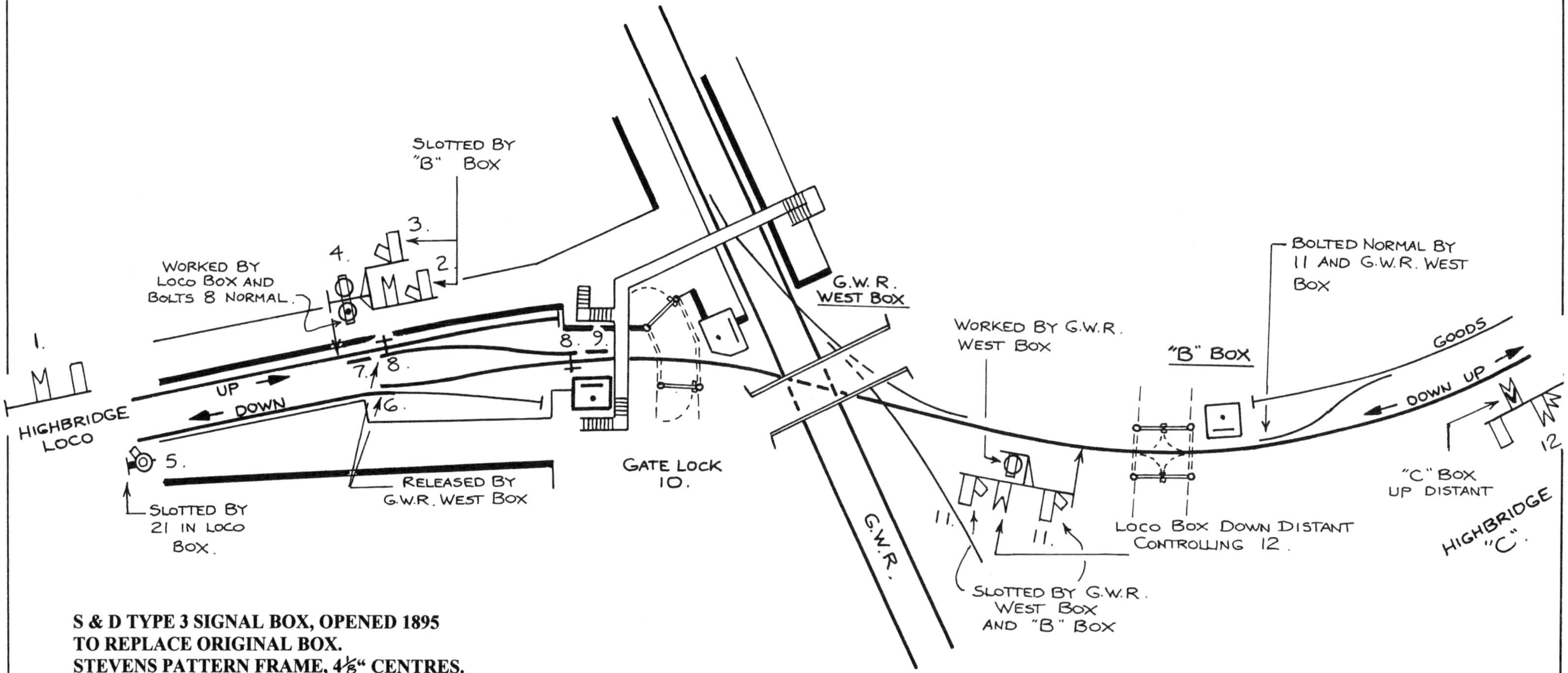

1.
HIGHBRIDGE LOCO
WORKED BY LOCO BOX AND BOLTS 8 NORMAL.
4.
SLOTTED BY "B" BOX
3.
2.
UP
DOWN
5.
SLOTTED BY 21 IN LOCO BOX.
7.
8.
6.
RELEASED BY G.W.R. WEST BOX
8.
9.
GATE LOCK 10.
G.W.R. WEST BOX
G.W.R.
WORKED BY G.W.R. WEST BOX
11.
11.
SLOTTED BY G.W.R. WEST BOX AND "B" BOX
"B" BOX
LOCO BOX DOWN DISTANT CONTROLLING 12.
BOLTED NORMAL BY 11 AND G.W.R. WEST BOX
GOODS
DOWN
UP
"C" BOX UP DISTANT
12
HIGHBRIDGE "C".

S & D TYPE 3 SIGNAL BOX, OPENED 1895
TO REPLACE ORIGINAL BOX.
STEVENS PATTERN FRAME, 4⅛" CENTRES.
BLOCK TELEGRAPH TO HIGHBRIDGE LOCO.
"NO TABLET" BELL BLOCK TO GWR WEST AND HIGHBRIDGE "B" BOXES.
CLOSING SWITCH:- NIL.

BOX CLOSED 1914 AND WORK TRANSFERRED TO GWR WEST BOX.

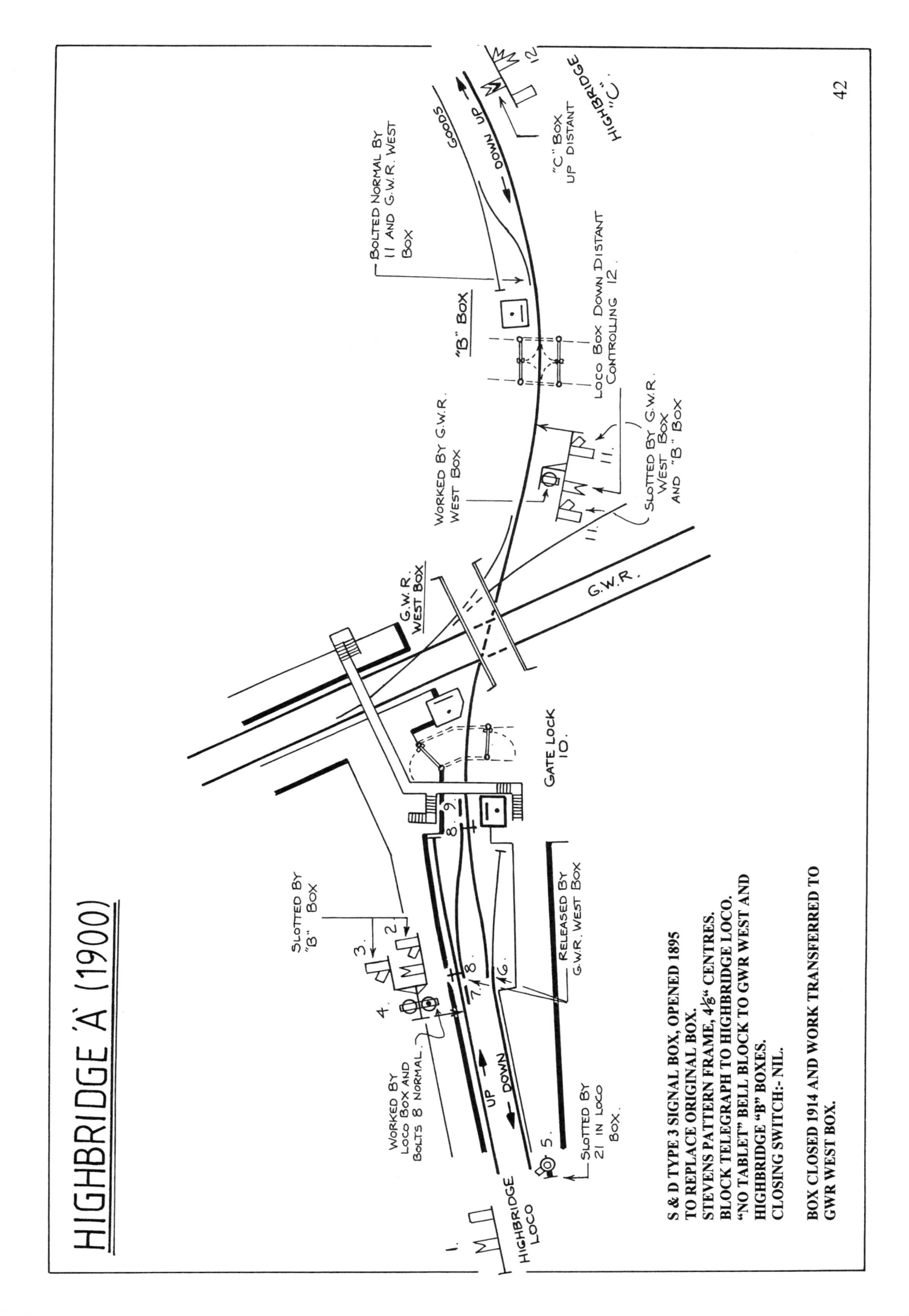

HIGHBRIDGE LOCO (1895)

RENAMED "HIGHBRIDGE 'A'" c. 1935 AND "HIGHBRIDGE EAST 'C'" 1949.

S & D TYPE 2 SIGNAL BOX, OPENED MARCH 1895.
STEVENS FRAME, 4⅛" CENTRES, 23 LEVERS, EXTENDED
TO 25 LEVERS NOVEMBER 1896.
FPL STANDS NORMALLY "OUT".
BLOCK TELEGRAPH TO HIGHBRIDGE "A" UNTIL 1914, THEN
GWR DISC BLOCK TO WEST BOX.
TRAIN STAFF & TICKET TO EDINGTON JUNCTION, REPLACED
WITH TYER'S No. 1 TABLET.
CLOSING SWITCH:- NIL.

SPARE : 19 :

* WORKED BY G.W.R WEST BOX FROM 1914.

23. Controls "A" Box Up Distant

HIGHBRIDGE EAST 'C' (1955)

NOTES ON SIGNAL BOX AND EQUIPMENT AS PER DIAGRAM ON PREVIOUS PAGE.
TYER'S No. 6 TABLET TO SHAPWICK (FOLLOWING CLOSURE OF EDINGTON JCN) FROM 04-02-1956. ELECTRIC KEY TOKEN FROM c. 1960

CARRIAGE SIDINGS (POINTS 20 AND DISCS 19 PULL & 19 PUSH) ADDED IN 1896. WAR DEPARTMENT SIDINGS (POINTS 25, DISCS 22 PULL & 22 PUSH AND TRACK CIRCUIT 'A') ADDED c. 1943.

TYER'S No. 6 TABLET REPLACED BY ELECTRIC KEY TOKEN c.1962 THROUGH TO SHAPWICK (EDINGTON JCN. ALREADY CLOSED).

WAR DEPARTMENT SIDINGS REMOVED 1964

Box Open (1960)
06.15 to 22.30 (Mon. to Sat.)
15.00 to 19.00 (Sundays)

BOX CLOSED 06-03-1966.

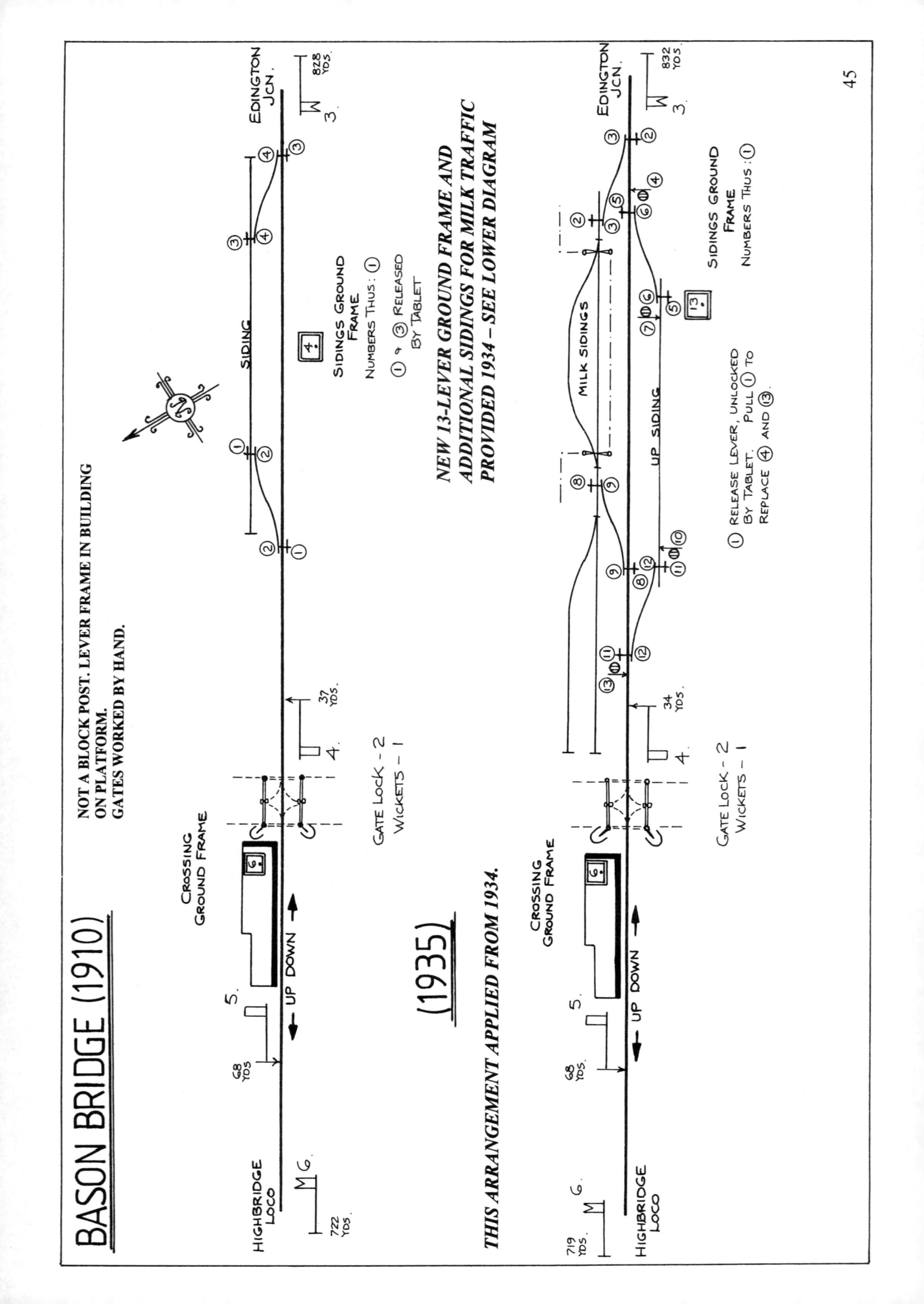

BASON BRIDGE (1910)

NOT A BLOCK POST. LEVER FRAME IN BUILDING ON PLATFORM. GATES WORKED BY HAND.

Sidings Ground Frame
Numbers thus: ①
① & ③ Released by Tablet

Gate Lock – 2
Wickets – 1

(1935)

NEW 13-LEVER GROUND FRAME AND ADDITIONAL SIDINGS FOR MILK TRAFFIC PROVIDED 1934 – SEE LOWER DIAGRAM

THIS ARRANGEMENT APPLIED FROM 1934.

Sidings Ground Frame
Numbers thus: ①

① Release lever, unlocked by tablet. Pull ① to replace ④ and ③.

Gate Lock – 2
Wickets – 1

EDINGTON JUNCTION (1891)

DUTTON TYPE 1 SIGNAL BOX, OPENED JUNE 1890.
DUTTON'S PATENT LEVER FRAME.
FPLs STAND NORMALLY "OUT".
GATES WORKED BY HAND.
TRAIN STAFF & TICKET ON MAIN LINES.
TYER'S No. 3 TABLET ON BRANCH.

GATE LOCK – 34.
WICKETS – 35.
GATES WORKED BY HAND.

SPARE: 20; 25; 27.

DUTTON FRAME REPLACED BY ONE OF STEVENS TYPE c.1915 – SEE BELOW.

(1920)

STEVENS PATTERN FRAME, 4⅛" CENTRES.
TYER'S No. 1 TABLET TO HIGHBRIDGE LOCO.
TYER'S No. 3 TABLET TO SHAPWICK & BRIDGWATER.
FPLs STAND NORMALLY "OUT" EXCEPT THOSE ON POINTS 16b AND 26b WHICH ARE FITTED WITH ECONOMIC LOCKS AND STAND BOLTED.

GATE LOCK – 38.
WICKETS – 39.
GATES WORKED BY HAND.

SPARE: 6; 12; 13; 14; 15; 30.

BOX CLOSED 04-02-1956. GROUND FRAME PROVIDED FOR SIDING POINTS BUT EVERYTHING ELSE TAKEN OUT OF USE.

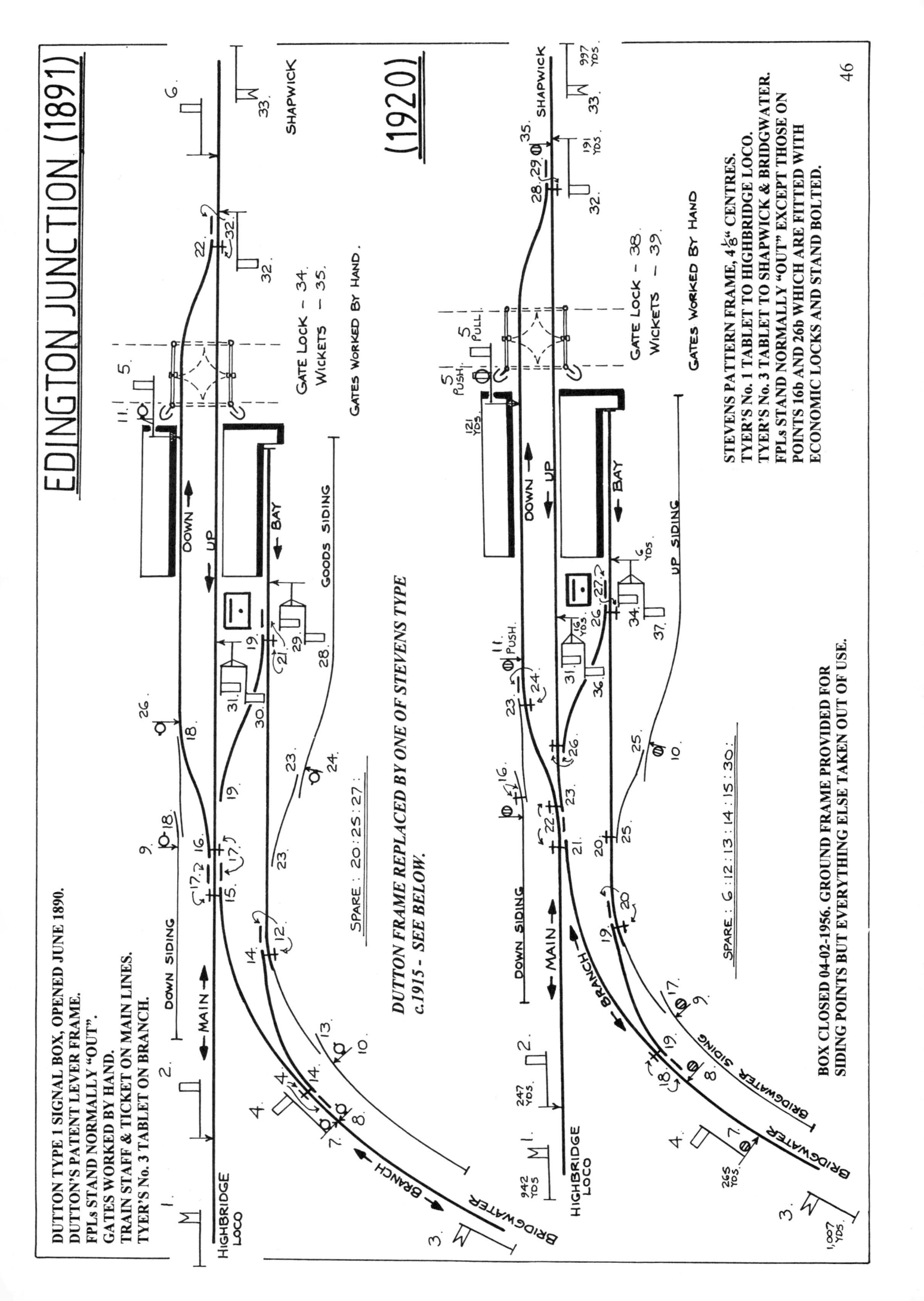

46

SHAPWICK (1910)

NOTE: 12 PULL, WHEN PULLED, ALSO TAKES OFF 12 PUSH.

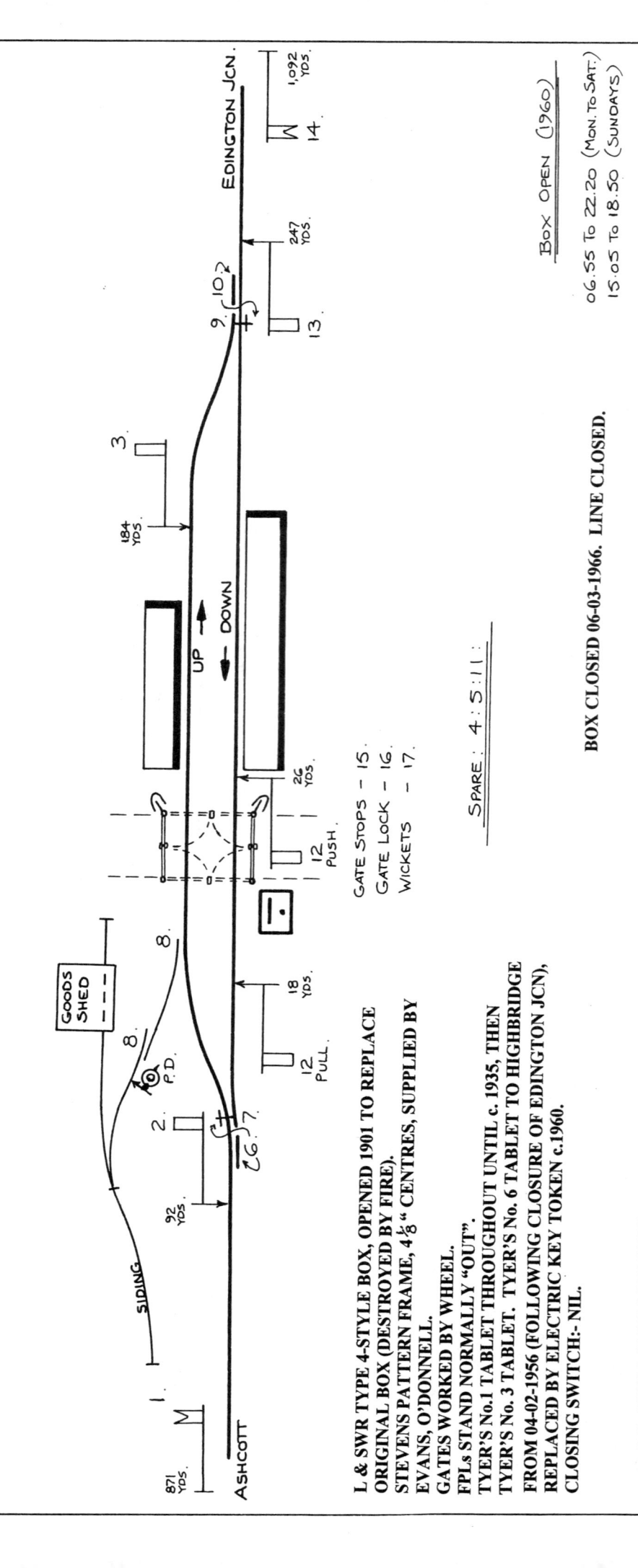

ASHCOTT ← → EDINGTON JCN.

Gate Stops – 15.
Gate Lock – 16.
Wickets – 17.

Spare: 4 : 5 : 11 :

Box Open (1960)

06.55 to 22.20 (Mon. to Sat.)
15.05 to 18.50 (Sundays)

BOX CLOSED 06-03-1966. LINE CLOSED.

L & SWR TYPE 4-STYLE BOX, OPENED 1901 TO REPLACE ORIGINAL BOX (DESTROYED BY FIRE).
STEVENS PATTERN FRAME, 4⅛" CENTRES, SUPPLIED BY EVANS, O'DONNELL.
GATES WORKED BY WHEEL.
FPLs STAND NORMALLY "OUT".
TYER'S No.1 TABLET THROUGHOUT UNTIL c. 1935, THEN TYER'S No. 3 TABLET. TYER'S No. 6 TABLET TO HIGHBRIDGE FROM 04-02-1956 (FOLLOWING CLOSURE OF EDINGTON JCN), REPLACED BY ELECTRIC KEY TOKEN c.1960.
CLOSING SWITCH:- NIL.

28-05-1912: SIGNAL 12 PULL REMOVED AND SIGNAL 12 PUSH NOW SIMPLY 12 (PUSH & PULL ACTION OF LEVER ABOLISHED).

SIDING POINTS 8 ABOLISHED 1964.

47

ASHCOTT

SHAPWICK ← 910 YDS.

GLASTONBURY & STREET → 951 YDS.

GATE LOCK – G
WICKETS – 3

SPARE : 7 :

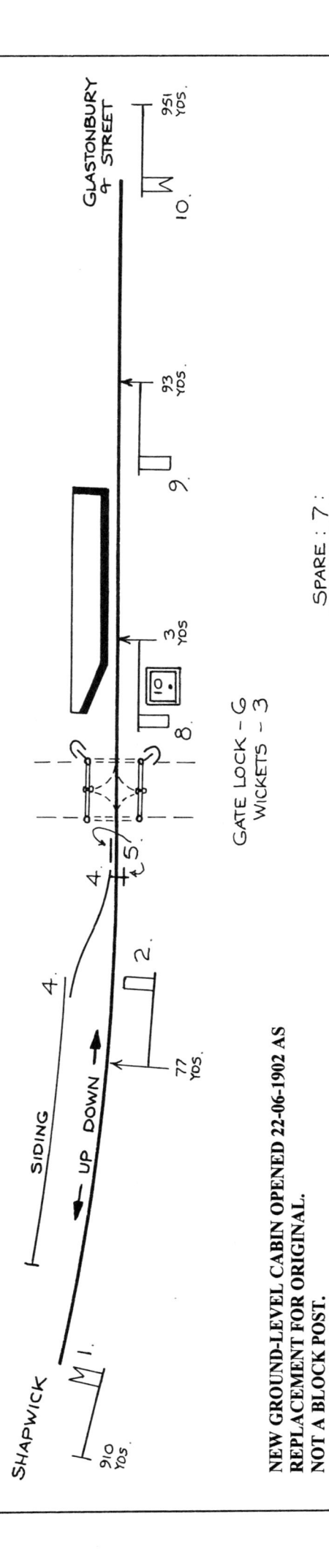

NEW GROUND-LEVEL CABIN OPENED 22-06-1902 AS REPLACEMENT FOR ORIGINAL. NOT A BLOCK POST.

F.P.L. 5 RELEASED BY TABLET, STANDS NORMALLY "IN", AND LOCKS FOR MAIN LINE ONLY.

CLOSED 06-03-1966. LINE CLOSED.

GLASTONBURY AND STREET

L & SWR TYPE 4-STYLE WOODEN SIGNAL BOX, OPENED 03-06-1901 TO REPLACE ORIGINAL. STEVENS PATTERN FRAME, 4⅞" CENTRES. FPLs STAND NORMALLY "OUT". TYER'S No. 3 TABLET TO SHAPWICK. TYER'S No. 1 TABLET TO WEST PENNARD AND WELLS. WORKING TO WEST PENNARD ALTERED TO ELECTRIC KEY TOKEN c. 1960. CLOSING SWITCH:- NIL.

29-10-1951: WELLS BRANCH CLOSED. SIGNALS 4, 5, AND 23 REMOVED AND TRAP POINTS 9 WITH DISCS 20 PULL & 20 PUSH ABOLISHED. 'A' END OF 16 POINTS RETAINED AS TRAP. TYER'S No. 1 INSTRUMENT TO WELLS RECOVERED.

BOX CLOSED 06-03-1966. LINE CLOSED.

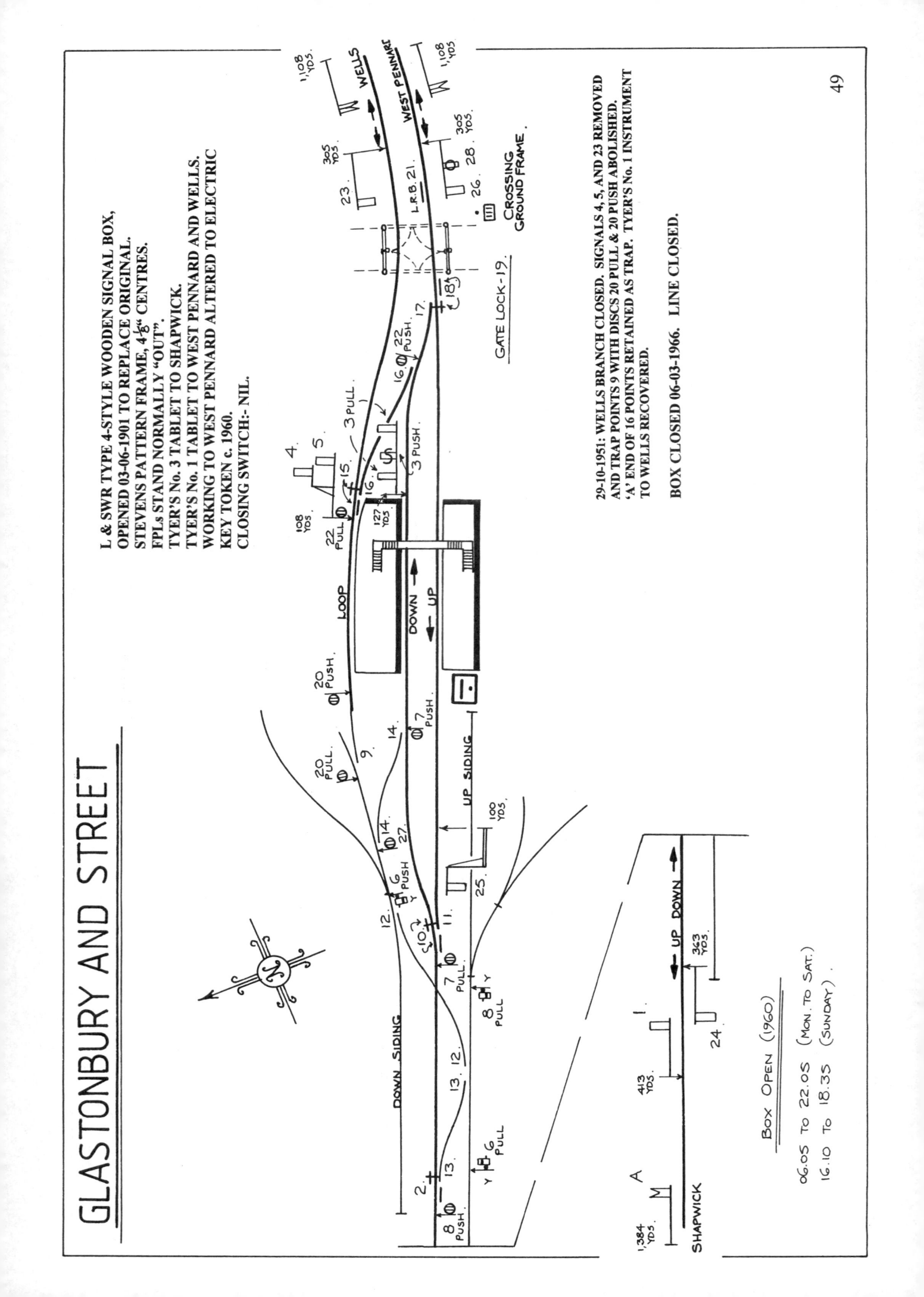

Box Open (1960)
06.05 to 22.05 (Mon. to Sat.)
16.10 to 18.35 (Sunday).

49

WEST PENNARD (1900)

TYPE OF BOX AND DATE OF OPENING UNCERTAIN. STEVENS FRAME, 4⅛" CENTRES. FPL 15 STANDS NORMALLY "OUT". POINTS 10 FITTED WITH ECONOMIC LOCK AND STAND NORMALLY BOLTED. TYER'S No. 1 TABLET, TO GLASTONBURY, ALTERED c.1960 TO ELECTRIC KEY TOKEN. TYER'S No. 1 TABLET TO PYLLE REPLACED BY TYER'S No. 3 TABLET TO EVERCREECH JCN. NORTH WHEN PYLLE BOX CLOSED IN 1929.

SPARE : 7 : 8 : 9 : 16 :

CONNECTIONS TO SIDINGS ALTERED 1929 – SEE BELOW.

(1930)

NOTES ON SIGNAL BOX AND EQUIPMENT AS PER UPPER DIAGRAM EXCEPT THAT TYER'S No. 3 INSTRUMENT TO EVERCREECH JUNCTION NORTH REPLACED BY ELECTRIC KEY TOKEN c. 1960.

BOX CLOSED 06-03-1966. LINE CLOSED.

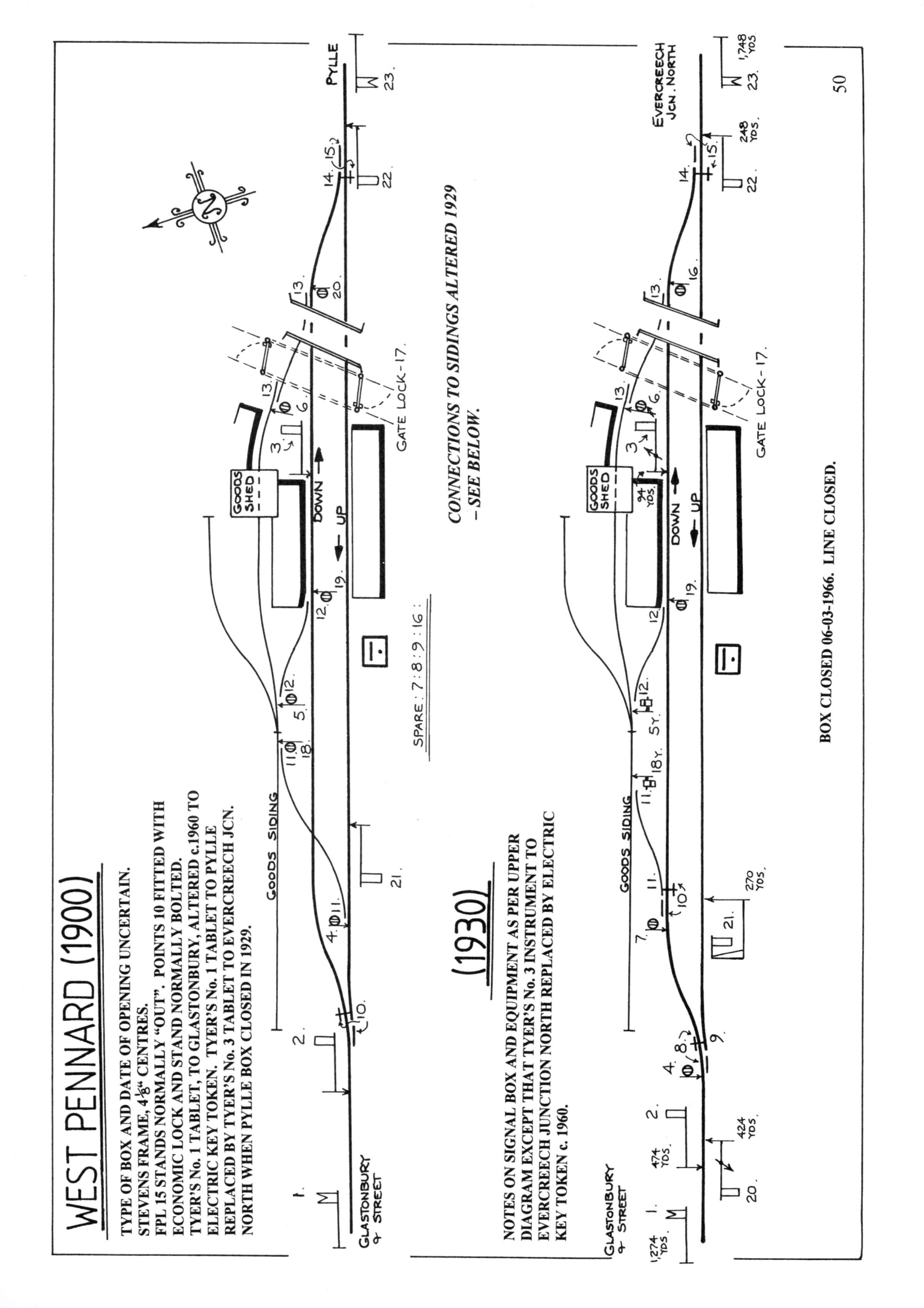

PYLLE (1891)

S & D TYPE 1 SIGNAL BOX, ERECTED 1877.
RELOCKED 1891 AND NEW CROSSING PLACE BROUGHT INTO USE.
TYER'S No. 1 TABLET TO WEST PENNARD.
TYER'S No. 3 TABLET TO EVERCREECH JCN.
CLOSING SWITCH;- NIL.
POINTS 8 AND 11 FITTED WITH BLACK'S ECONOMIC LOCKS AND STAND NORMALLY BOLTED.

GATE LOCK - 7. GATES WORKED BY HAND.

SPARE : 6 : 12 :

LOOP REMOVED AND BOX REDUCED TO GROUND FRAME (FOR SIDING POINTS) 08-12-1929.

CLOSED 21-06-1964 WHEN SIDING TAKEN OUT OF USE.

51

SECTION THREE

BRIDGWATER BRANCH

OPENED
21-07-1890

CLOSED
29-10-1951 (Passengers)
04-10-1954 (Goods)

BRIDGWATER (NORTH)

"NORTH" SUFFIX ADDED 1949.

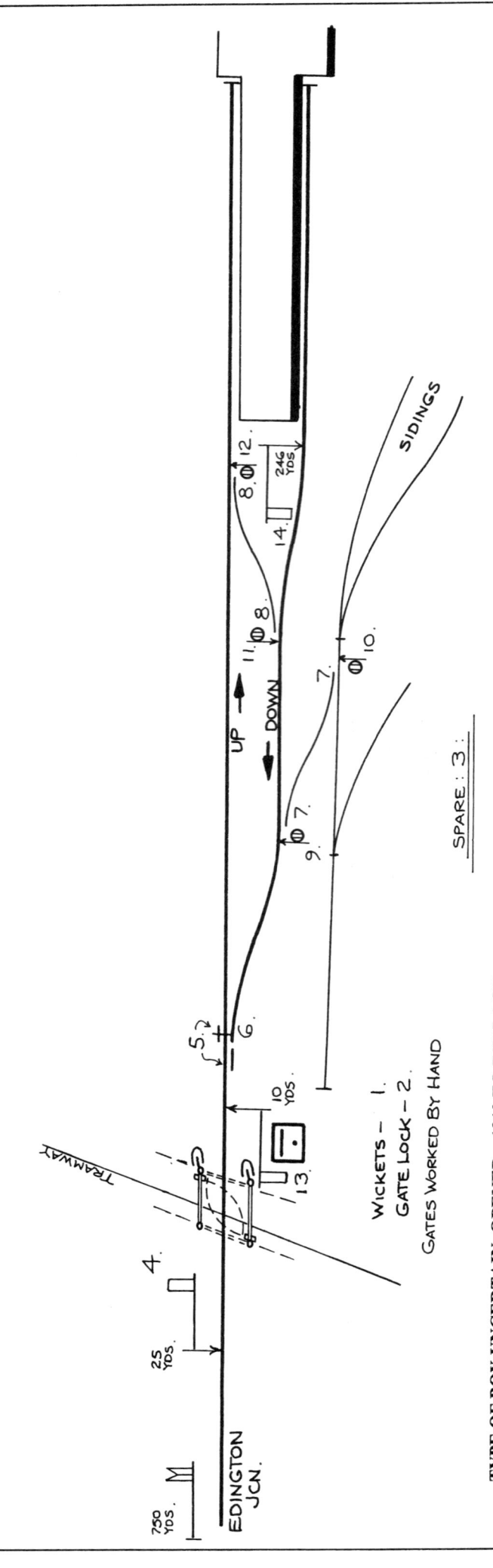

TYPE OF BOX UNCERTAIN. OPENED c.1910 TO REPLACE
ORIGINAL DUTTON EQUIPMENT.
GROUND-LEVEL STEVENS FRAME, $4\frac{5}{8}$" CENTRES.
FPL STANDS NORMALLY "OUT".
TYER'S No. 3 TABLET.
GATES WORKED BY HAND.
CLOSING SWITCH:- NIL.

WICKETS - 1.
GATE LOCK - 2.
GATES WORKED BY HAND

SPARE : 3.

BOX CLOSED 04-10-1954.

LINE TO EDINGTON CLOSED AND NEW CHORD
(FOR GOODS TRAFFIC ONLY) PROVIDED TO
CONNECT WITH FORMER GWR DOCKS BRANCH.
POINTS CONVERTED TO HAND OPERATION.

COSSINGTON

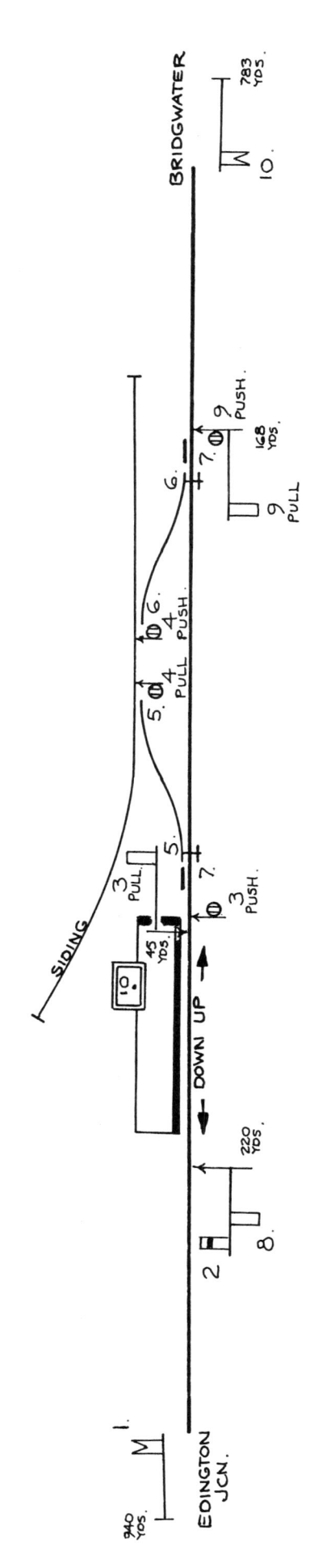

PLATFORM-LEVEL CABIN: NOT A BLOCK POST.
FPLs STAND NORMALLY "IN" AND LEVER 7 RELEASED
BY TABLET FOR EDINGTON JCN. – BRIDGWATER SECTION.

DATE OF ABOLITION NOT RECORDED.

SECTION FOUR
WELLS BRANCH

OPENED
15-03-1859

CLOSED
29-10-1951 (Completely)

POLSHAM

OPENED 1891, BUT NOT A BLOCK POST AND LITTLE INFORMATION IS AVAILABLE.
LEVER 3 RELEASED BY TABLET FOR WELLS – GLASTONBURY SECTION, AND FPL STANDS NORMALLY "IN".

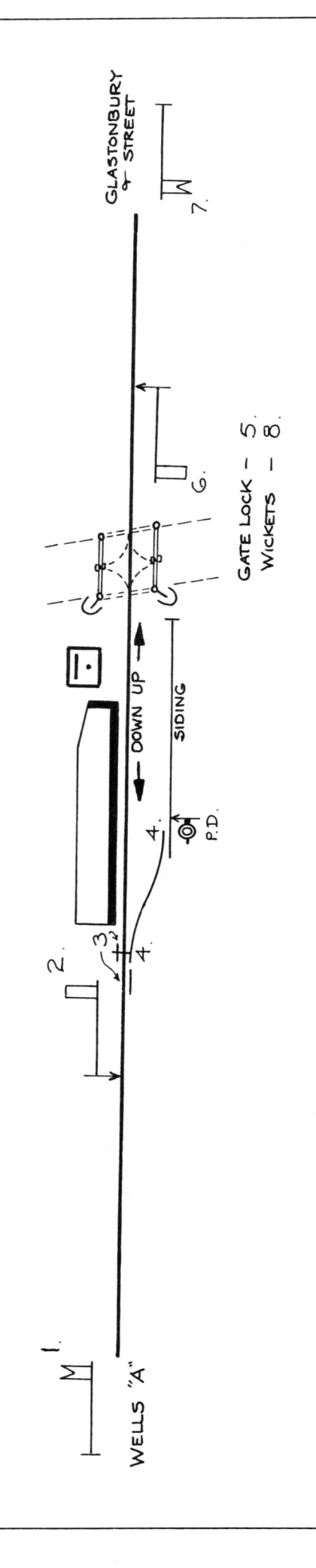

CLOSED 29-10-1951. LINE CLOSED.

Gate Lock – 5.
Wickets – 8.

WELLS 'A' (1920)

S & D NON-STANDARD STONE BOX. DATE OF OPENING AND
TYPE OF LEVER FRAME NOT RECORDED.
TYER'S No. 1 TABLET TO GLASTONBURY.
"NO TOKEN" BLOCK ON G.W.R. LINES.
CLOSING SWITCH: NIL UNTIL 1930 (SEE NEXT PAGE).
FPLs 11, 12, & 22 STAND NORMALLY "OUT".
FPLs 20, 23, & 24 STAND NORMALLY "IN".

06.09.1910 :- ARMS 1 AND 2 REMOVED. (6, 7, 28 & 31 FIXED AT DANGER).

CONNECTIONS TO YARD ALTERED c. 1921
— SEE NEXT PAGE.

57

WELLS 'A' (1931)

NOTES ON SIGNAL BOX AND EQUIPMENT AS PER PREVIOUS PAGE EXCEPT THAT CLOSING SWITCH IS NOW PROVIDED (FOR G.W.R. LINE).

SPECIAL: To Close Box Pull Closing Switch Half Way, Which Releases No. 28. 28 Pulled Releases Second Half of Closing Switch.

Closing Switch "Out" Locks 28 Over.

NEW LEVER FRAME INSTALLED 02-10-1949 — SEE NEXT PAGE.

SPARE: 1 : 2 : 6 : 7 : 23 : 24 : 31.

27. When Switch "In"
28. When Switch "Out"

WELLS 'A' (1950)

Spare: 12 ; 13 ; 14 :

Closing Switch Pulled Halfway Releases 16.
16 Pulled Releases Second Half of Switch.
When Box Closed Line set For G.W.R.

NEW WESTINGHOUSE 'A2' FRAME, 4" CENTRES, INSTALLED
IN EXISTING SIGNAL BOX. INTO USE 02-10-1949.
ALL OTHER DETAILS AS PER PREVIOUS DRAWINGS.

BOX CLOSED 02-12-1955 AND GROUND FRAME PROVIDED TO
CONTROL SIDING POINTS.

59